How To
Understand the
Book of
Isaiah

From the
Library of:

Seek ye the Lord while he may be found, call ye upon him while he is near:

Let the wicked forsake his way, and the unrighteous man his thoughts: and let him return unto the Lord, and he will have mercy upon him; and to our God, for he will abundantly pardon.

For my thoughts are not your thoughts, neither are your ways my ways, saith the Lord.

For as the heavens are higher than the earth, so are my ways higher than your ways, and my thoughts than your thoughts.

(Isaiah 55:6-9)

How To Understand the Book of Isaiah

Duane S. Crowther

First Printing: September, 1998

Library of Congress Catalog Card Number
98-73536

International Standard Book Number
0-88290-635-6

Horizon Publishers' Catalog and Order Number:
1506

Printed and distributed
in the United States of America by

& Distributors, Incorporated

Mailing Address:
P.O. Box 490
Bountiful, Utah 84011-0490

Street Address:
50 South 500 West
Bountiful, Utah 84010

Local Phone: (801) 295-9451
WATS (toll free): 1 (800) 453-0812
FAX: (801) 295-0196

E-mail: horizonp@burgoyne.com
Internet: http:// www.horizonpublishers.com

Books by the Author

Religion

America—God's Chosen Land of Liberty

Atlas and Outline of the Acts of the Apostles

Atlas and Outline of the Life of Christ

Come Unto Christ

A Comprehensive Harmony of the Gospels

*Doctrinal Dimensions—Major Missionary Messages
of the Restored Gospel*

Gifts of the Spirit

God and His Church

A Guide to Effective Scripture Study

How to Understand the Book of Daniel

How to Understand the Book of Ezekiel

How to Understand the Book of Isaiah

How to Understand the Book of Jeremiah

How to Understand the Book of Mormon

How To Write Your Personal History

Inspired Prophetic Warnings

The Joy of Being a Woman

Life Everlasting—A Definitive Study of Life After Death

*The Life of Joseph Smith—An Atlas,
Chronological Outline and Documentation Harmony*

My Family Heritage—Adult Personal History Starter Kit

*A Personal History Journal For LDS Youth—
from Birth Through High School*

The Plan of Salvation and the Future in Prophecy

La Profecía—Llave al Futuro

The Prophecies of Joseph Smith—Over 400 Prophecies
By and About Joseph Smith and Their Fulfillment

Prophecy—Key to the Future

Prophetic Warnings to Modern America

Prophets and Prophecies of the Old Testament

A Study of Eschatological Prophecies Found in the Scriptures and the
Works of General Authorities of The Church of Jesus Christ
of Latter-day Saints (MA Thesis, Brigham Young University)

This Is My Life—Youth Genealogy Starter Kit

Thus Saith the Lord

La Vida Sempiterna

Music

Choral Concepts—Student Learning Guide, Units 1-4

Choral Concepts—Teachers Edition, Units 1-4

Fundamentals of Artistic Singing

A Model Program for In-Rehearsal Teaching of Choral Concepts
to High School Training Choirs
(Doctoral Dissertation, University of Utah)

Music Reading: Quick and Easy—A Singer's Guide

Teaching Choral Concepts

Teaching Choral Concepts—Instructor's Kit

Writing

Database Development for a New Products Master Plan
for Horizon Publishers and Distributors, Inc.
(MBA Thesis, University of Phoenix)

Book Marketing—Basic Industry Practices

Book Publishing—Basic Industry Practices

Expository Writing—Publication Evaluation Criteria
for Book Publishers, Agents and Authors

*Fiction Writing—Publication Evaluation Criteria
for Book Publishers, Agents and Authors*

Manuscript Publication Selection Criteria for Book Publishers

Subject-matter Trend Analysis of Best-selling Religious Books

Subject-matter Trend Analysis of Best-selling Trade Books

*Write With Power and Confidence—Writing Techniques and
Book-Industry Practices Every Author Should Know*

Cassette Talk Tapes by the Author

*Anarchy in America—Prophecies of Events
Preceding the Establishment of the New Jerusalem*

*Are You Saved?—A Mormon's View of
Faith, Works, Grace, and Salvation*

Armageddon

Biblical Proofs of the Book of Mormon

Biblical Proofs of the Restored Church

*Doctrinal Evidences that Mormons Are Christians—A Refutation of
Misleading Statements Circulated by Anti-Mormon Critics*

Exaltation and the Kingdoms of Glory

Forty Keys to Family Emergency Readiness

*From First Draft to First Edition—A Step-by-Step Guide
to Self-Publishing*

God Speaks Through Prophets Today

God's Eternal Plan of Salvation

The Great and Abominable Church in Prophecy

*He Comes in Glory—The Second Coming of Jesus Christ
and Events Prophesied to Precede It*

How To Recognize Spiritual Promptings

How To Seek the Gifts of the Spirit

Interpreting the Book of Revelation

Israel—Past, Present and Future

Joseph Smith—A True Prophet of God

A Latter-day Saint View of Christ and the Trinity

Missionary and Temple Work for the Dead

Nephi's Panoramic Preview—2,500 Years in Prophecy

The New Jerusalem and the Council at Adam-ondi-Ahman

Paradise—The Spirit-world Home of the Righteous

Recognizing Techniques of Deception in Anti-Mormon Literature

The Resurrection—Doctrine, History and Prophecy

*Seeking the Gifts of Church Leadership—Administration,
Diversities of Operations and Discerning of Spirits*

*Seeking the Gifts of Communication—Revelation, Prophecy, Speaking in
Tongues, Interpretation of Tongues, and Self-Expression: Speaking,
Writing, Translation, Teaching,
Expounding the Scriptures and Bearing Testimony*

*Seeking the Gifts of Faith,
Healing, Miracles, Helps and Governments*

Seeking the Gifts of Testimony, Knowledge and Wisdom

*Seeking the Gifts of Salvation and Exaltation—
Repentance, Charity, Hope and Eternal Life*

Through Death Unto Life Everlasting

Understanding Isaiah in the Book of Mormon

Why Join the Mormons?

World War III—God's Judgments Upon the Nations

Ye Must Be Born Again

Contents

Part 1

Part ll

Part III

Part IV

Part 1

ISAIAH
HIS WRITINGS
AND
HIS TIMES

The sinners in Zion are afraid; fearfulness hath surprised the hypocrites. Who among us shall dwell with the devouring fire? who among us shall dwell with everlasting burnings?

He that walketh righteously, and speaketh uprightly; he that despiseth the gain of oppressions, that shaketh his hands from holding of bribes, that stoppeth his ears from hearing of blood, and shutteth his eyes from seeing evil;

He shall dwell on high: his place of defence shall be the munitions of rocks: bread shall be given him; his waters shall be sure.

(Isaiah 33:14-16)

In those days was Hezekiah sick unto death. And Isaiah the prophet the son of Amoz came unto him, and said unto him, Thus saith the LORD, Set thine house in order: for thou shalt die, and not live.

Then Hezekiah turned his face toward the wall, and prayed unto the LORD,

And said, Remember now, O LORD, I beseech thee, how I have walked before thee in truth and with a perfect heart, and have done that which is good in thy sight. And Hezekiah wept sore.

Then came the word of the LORD to Isaiah, saying,

Go, and say to Hezekiah, Thus saith the LORD, the God of David thy father, I have heard thy prayer, I have seen thy tears: behold, I will add unto thy days fifteen years.

And I will deliver thee and this city out of the hand of the king of Assyria: and I will defend this city.

And this shall be a sign unto thee from the LORD, that the LORD will do this thing that he hath spoken;

Behold, I will bring again the shadow of the degrees, which is gone down in the sun dial of Ahaz, ten degrees backward. So the sun returned ten degrees, by which degrees it was gone down.

(Isaiah 38:1-8)

1

INFORMATION ABOUT ISAIAH AND HIS TIMES

Prophet's Name

Isaiah (i sā´ uh), means "Jehovah has saved."

Scriptural Information About the Prophet

1. He was a son of Amoz (not Amos the prophet). (1:1)

2. He preached during the reigns of Uzziah, Jotham, Ahaz and Hezekiah, kings of Judah. (1:1)

3. He preached actively to the kings of Judah during two crises of Judah:

A. *The Syro-Ephraimite War* (c. 734 B.C.) in which Pekah (king of Israel) and Rezin (king of Syria) attempted to force Ahaz (king of Judah) to ally Judah with them against Assyria. (Chapters 7-8)

B. *The Assyrian attack under Sennacherib* (c. 701 B.C.). The Assyrian hosts were smitten by the Lord and departed with heavy losses. (Chapters 36-37)

4. Isaiah's family:

A. *Wife:* Her name is not known. She was a prophetess. (8:3)

B. *Son:* Maher-shalal-hash-baz (Mā´-hĕr-shăl´-ăl-hăsh´-băz), means "the spoil speedeth, the prey hasteth." (8:3)

C. *Son:* Shear-jashub (Shē´-är-jăsh´-ub), means "a remnant shall return." (7:3)

D. *Family mission:* "Behold, I and the children whom the Lord hath given me are for signs and for wonders in Israel from the Lord of hosts, which dwelleth in mount Zion." (8:18)

5. Isaiah received his call as a prophet in the last year of king Uzziah's reign. (6:1)

6. *Other books were written by Isaiah* which have not been preserved:

A. A life of Uzziah. (2 Chron. 26:22)

B. The Book of the Kings of Judah and Israel. (2 Chron. 32:32)

7. *Book of Mormon references to Isaiah* show his greatness as a prophet:

A. "I did read unto them that which was written by the prophet Isaiah; for I did liken all scriptures unto us, that it might be for our profit and learning." (1 Ne. 19:23)

B. "And now I, Nephi, write more of the words of Isaiah, for my soul delighteth in his words. For I will liken his words unto my people, and I will send them forth unto all my children, for he verily saw my Redeemer, even as I have seen him." (2 Ne. 11:2)

C. "Isaiah spake many things which were hard for many of my people to understand; for they know not concerning the manner of prophesying among the Jews." (2 Ne. 25:1)

D. ". . . because the words of Isaiah are not plain unto you, nevertheless they are plain unto all those that are filled with the spirit of prophecy." (2 Ne. 25:4)

E. ". . . in the days that the prophecies of Isaiah shall be fulfilled men shall know of a surety, at the times when they shall come to pass." (2 Ne. 25:7)

F. "Ye remember that I spake unto you, and said that when the words of Isaiah should be fulfilled—behold they are written, ye have them before you, therefore search them—And verily, verily, I say unto you, that when they shall be fulfilled then is the fulfilling of the covenant which the Father made unto his people, O house of Israel." (3 Ne. 20:11-12)

G. "And now, behold, I say unto you, that ye ought to search these things. Yea, a commandment I give unto you that ye search these things diligently; for great are the words of Isaiah. For surely he spake as touching all things concerning my people which are of the house of Israel; therefore it must needs be that he must speak also to the Gentiles. And all things that he spake have been and shall be, even according to the words which he spake." (3 Ne. 23:1-3)

H. "And I did rehearse unto them the words of Isaiah, who spake concerning the restoration of the Jews, or of the house of Israel; and after they were restored they should no more be confounded, neither should they be scattered again." (1 Ne. 15:20)

I. Search the prophecies of Isaiah. Behold, I cannot write them" (Morm. 8:23)

8. There are two traditions about Isaiah:

A. Rabbinic tradition says that Isaiah's father was a brother to king Amaziah. If this was true, then Isaiah was a cousin of king Uzziah and therefore of royal blood.

B. A tradition in the Talmud says that Isaiah was martyred by being tied to two planks and then being sawed asunder with a wooden saw. (Heb. 11:37?)

Date of Isaiah's Mission

c. 740-697 B.C.

1. He began his ministry in the year King Uzziah (of Judah) died (c. 740 B.C.). (6:1)

2. He preached during the reigns of four kings of Judah: Uzziah and Jotham (c. 740-734 B.C.); Ahaz (c. 734-728 B.C.); and Hezekiah (c. 728-697 B.C.). (1:1)

Prophesied to

Israel and **Judah**

Contemporary Prophets

Hosea	c. 760-720 B.C.	to Israel.
Micah	c. 740-697 B.C.	to Israel and Judah.

Contemporary Prophets Contrasted

Isaiah is a statesman and a member of Jerusalem's ruling class. He is well acquainted with the society and political intrigues of the capital city of Jerusalem and shows much interest in the political events of his time. He is a capable author and speaker. His writing reflects his culture and refinement.

Hosea gives a more intimate view of his personal affairs in his writing than any of the other prophets except Jeremiah. He was a man who suffered many hardships to keep the Lord's commandments. His writing is highly emotional and less objective than the writing of his contemporaries. His fervor substitutes for stylistic dignity.

   Micah is a product of the open hills and shows dislike for the cities. (See Micah 1:5, 5:11, 6:9.) As a member of the oppressed peasantry he speaks for the common people and defends them against the nobles and rich landlords of Judah. He is primarily an ethical and religious teacher and shows little knowledge or interest in political matters.

Contemporary Kings

Israel:

Menahem	c. 748-737 B.C.

Paid tribute to Tiglath-Pileser III to save Israel.

Pekahiah	c. 737-735 B.C.
Pekah	c. 735-733 B.C.

Israel and Syria attacked Judah in 734 B.C.

Hoshea	c. 733-722 B.C.

Fall of the Kingdom of Israel c. 722 B.C.

Judah:

Uzziah	c. 792-740 B.C.
Jotham	c. 749-734 B.C.
Ahaz	c. 734-728 B.C.

Formed an alliance with Assyria against Israel and Syria. Judah was defeated by Israel and Syria in 734 B.C. but the Jewish captives were returned.

Hezekiah	c. 728-697 B.C.

He was attacked by Sennacherib in 701 B.C. but was saved when 185,000 Assyrians died.

Manasseh	c. 697-642 B.C.

Assyria:

Tiglath-Pileser III	c. 745-727 B.C.

Overran northern Israel in 733 B.C.

Shalmaneser V	c. 726-722 B.C.

Laid siege to Samaria, capital of Israel in 722 B.C. He died during the siege.

Sargon II	c. 721-705 B.C.

Completed the conquest of Israel. Deported the Ten Tribes in 721 B.C.

Sennacherib	c. 704-681 B.C.

Attacked Judah in 701 B.C. He withdrew when 185,000 of his men died.

National Conditions—Israel and Judah

Political

1. Political decay was even more in evidence in Isaiah's time than noted previously.

2. Power had become concentrated in Jerusalem.

3. The city rulers oppressed the rural population with heavy taxation to support their policy of paying tribute to Assyria and to fortify the city of Jerusalem.

4. Corrupt judges aided their friends in robbing the poor. Bribes and intrigue were characteristic of most governmental and judicial decisions.

Economic

1. Greater social and moral decay than at previous times was found in Judah and Israel.

2. There was increased effort on the part of large landowners to evict small property owners and enlarge their estates.

3. High and unequal taxation, and foreclosures on credit, were the tools by which the poor were oppressed by the rich.

Religious

1. Following the early reforms of Hezekiah, men began to turn against the worship of Jehovah and assert that their religion had promised more than it could give.

2. Worshippers of Jehovah began to worship other gods. Their national impotence against Assyria seemed to indicate that other national gods existed and that they should seek the favor of these foreign gods.

3. National misfortunes were interpreted as indications of Jehovah's anger. They mistakenly attempted to appease this anger by observing pagan worship forms such as offering their children as sacrifices.

4. The terror of approaching destruction led the people to persecute those who worshiped only Jehovah and who would not seek the aid of pagan deities.

Notes on the Study and Interpretation of the Book of Isaiah

Isaiah is the largest book of the Bible. Its size and complexity make it very difficult to understand unless a systematic program for its study is adopted. The book is often given some form of the following general outline by Bible scholars.

General Outline of the Book of Isaiah

Part 1. Chapters 1-12—Prophecies concerning Judah.
Part 2. Chapters 13-23—Prophecies concerning Judah's neighbors.
Part 3. Chapters 24-27—Prophecies concerning a judgment on the world in the last days.
Part 4. Chapters 28-33—Prophecies concerning the future of Israel and discourses concerning the current relationship of Judah to Assyria.
Part 5. Chapters 34-35—Prophecies contrasting the future of Edom and Israel.
Part 6. Chapters 36-39—Historical section. Isaiah's activities during the reign of King Hezekiah.
Part 7. Chapters 40-66—Prophecies of Israel's future glory.

Such an outline is so broad that it offers little, if any, help to the student.

Most studies examine the writings of Isaiah from the standpoint of *when he talked.* While such an approach is useful for some purposes, it leaves many students in utter confusion. It would seem more logical to group Isaiah's writings for study purposes into categories determined by *to whom he talked* and *when his prophecies would come to pass.*

In this book the writings of Isaiah are considered in four different sections. Each section represents one of the four major periods of prophetic fulfillment into which almost all scriptural prophecy may be conveniently classified. Again, these periods do not represent the time when the prophet is speaking. Rather, they deal with the time when his teachings and prophecies are to come to pass.

The four periods of prophetic fulfillment are as follows:

Periods of Prophetic Fulfillment

1. **Events Before and During the Fall of Israel to Assyria—800-700 B.C.**

   A. **The reigns of—**

      1. Jeroboam II, Zachariah, Shallum, Menahem, Pekahiah, Pekah and Hoshea, kings of Israel.
      2. Uzziah, Jotham, Ahaz, and Hezekiah, kings of Judah.
      3. Adad-nirari III, Shalmaneser IV, Assur-Dayan III, Tiglath-Pileser III, Shalmaneser V, Sargon II, and Sennacherib, kings of Assyria.

   B. **Prophecies which primarily concern—**

      1. The above kings.
      2. Assyrian assaults on the Mediterranean States.
      3. Alliances with Egypt and Assyria.
      4. The Syro-Ephraimite War, c. 734 B.C.
      5. The fall of northern Israel, c. 733 B.C.
      6. The siege and fall of Samaria, c. 722 B.C.
      7. The deportation of the remainder of Israel, c. 721 B.C.
      8. Sennacherib's attacks on Judah in 701 B.C. and 698 B.C.

2. **Events Before and During the Fall of Judah, The Babylonian Captivity and the Jewish Return to Palestine (primarily 635-535 B.C.)**

   A. **The reigns of—**

      1. Manasseh, Amon, Josiah, Ahaziah, Jehoiakim, Jehoiachin, Zedekiah, and Gedeliah, *kings of Judah.*
      2. Nabopolassar, Nebuchadnezzar, Evil-Merodach, Nabonidus, and Belshazzar, *kings of Babylonia.*
      3. Cyrus II, Cambyses, and Darius I, *kings of Persia and Media.*

   B. **Prophecies which primarily concern—**

      1. The above kings.
      2. The Battle of Carchemish, 605 B.C.
      3. The fall of Nineveh and Assyria, c. 612 B.C.
      4. The first surrender of Jerusalem, under Jehoiachin, c. 598 BC.
      5. The fall of Jerusalem under Zedekiah, c. 588 B.C.
      6. The Babylonian captivity.
      7. The fall of Babylon and the coming of Cyrus, c. 538 B.C.
      8. The three returns from captivity: 636 B.C., 469 B.C., 444 B.C.

3. **Events Related to the Ministry of Christ (in the meridian of time)**

4. **Events During the Last Days (beginning with the restoration of the Gospel about 1820 A.D.)**

The book of Isaiah is open to many different interpretations by those of differing backgrounds and religions. It is recognized that some will disagree with the interpretative criteria by which the Latter-day Saints understand his writings. Be that as it may. For the purposes of this book, the author has divided the chapters of Isaiah into a study outline consisting of four sections, based on the four periods of prophetic fulfillment. It will be noted that the chapters are classified by their major message into one of the four groups. When a chapter makes reference to more than one period of prophetic fulfillment, the periods of the secondary items are indicated in the chapter outlines only.

The Book of Isaiah Divided, By Chapter, Into the Four Periods of Prophetic Fulfillment

Chapter	Outlined on page	Period I Israel, Judah, and Assyria	Period II Judah, Babylon, and the Captivity	Period III The Ministry of Christ	Period IV The Last Days
1	58		1		
2	88				2
3	59		3		
4	85				4
5	60		5		
6	47	6			
7	48	7			
8	49	8			
9	51	9			
10	58		10		
11	82				11
12	88				12
13	61		13		
14	62		14		
15	49	15			
16	49	16			
17	50	17			
18	78				18
19	50	19			

The Book of Isaiah Divided, By Chapter, Into the Four Periods of Prophetic Fulfillment

Chapter	Outlined on page	Period I — Israel, Judah, and Assyria	Period II — Judah, Babylon, and the Captivity	Period III — The Ministry of Christ	Period IV — The Last Days
20	50	20			
21	63		21		
22	52	22			
23	58		23		
24	90				24
25	92				25
26	90				26
27	81				27
28	52	28			
29	76				29
30	51	30			
31.	51	31			
32	92				32
33	91				33
34	91				34
35	81				35
36	54	36			
37	54	37			
38	53	38			
39	61		39		
40	88				40
41	63		41		
42	70			42	
43	64		43		
44	64		44		
45	64		45		
46	63		46		
47	63		47		
48	65		48		
49	79				49
50	72			50	

The Book of Isaiah Divided, By Chapter, Into the Four Periods of Prophetic Fulfillment

Chapter	Outlined on page	Period I — Israel, Judah, and Assyria	Period II — Judah, Babylon, and the Captivity	Period III — The Ministry of Christ	Period IV — The Last Days
51	84				51
52	80				52
53	72			53	
54	78				54
55	81				55
56	53	56			
57	53	57			
58	53	58			
59	53	59			
60	86				60
61	87				61
62	86				62
63	89				63
64	90				64
65	92				65
66	87				66

Woe unto them that seek deep to hide their counsel from the LORD, and their works are in the dark, and they say, Who seeth us? and who knoweth us?

Surely your turning of things upside down shall be esteemed as the potter's clay: for shall the work say of him that made it, He made me not? or shall the thing framed say of him that framed it, He had no understanding?

(Isaiah 29:15-16)

2

CRITICAL INFORMATION ABOUT THE BOOK OF ISAIAH

Style of the Book

1. Isaiah's writing is considered by many to be the finest in the Bible.
2. The book is partly in prose, and partly in poetry, as follows:

Prose	Poetry	Prose	Poetry	Prose	Poetry
1:1			14:24-27	27:12-13	
	1:2-31	14:28			28:1-29:10
2:1			14:29-16:11	29:11-12	
	2:2-3:17	16:12-14			29:13-30:18
3:18-23			17:1-6	30:19-26	
	3:24-26	17:7-9			30:27-28
4:1-6			17:10-19:15	30:29-33	
	5:1-30	19:16-20:6			31:1-5
6:1-8			21:1-15	31:6-7	
	6:9-13	21:16-17			31:8-35:10
7:1-6			22:1-8a	36:1-37:22a	
	7:7-11	22:8b-11			37:22a-29
7:12-8:8			22:12-14	37:30-38:9	
	8:9-10	22:15-25			38:10-20
8:11-9:1			23:1-12	38:21-39:8	
	9:2-10:11	23:13			40:1-44:8
10:12			23:14	44:9-20	
	10:13-19	23:15			44:21-52:2
10:20-27			23:16	52:3-6	
	10:28-11:9	23:17-18			52:7-59:20
11:10-11			24:1-25:5	59:21	
	11:12-13:22	25:6-12			60:1-66:16
14:1-3			26:1-21	66:17-21	
	14:4-21	27:1			66:22-23
14:22-23			27:2-11	66:24	

3. His poetry is rhythmic and makes full use of the complete array of Hebrew poetic techniques and figures of speech including:

    A. *Metaphor* (see for example, 1:13; 5:18, 22; 8:8; 10:22; 28:17, 20; 30:28, 30).

    B. *Paronomasia* [play on words] (see for example, 5:7; 7:9).

    C. *Antithesis* (see for example, 1:18; 3:24).

    D. *Alliteration* (see for example, 17:10, 12).

    E. *Hyperbole* and *parable* (see for example, 2:7; 5:1-7; 28:23-29).

    F. *Interrogation* (see for example, 10:8).

    G. *Dialogue* (see for example, 6:8) .

    H. *Personification* (see for example, 49:18-23; 51:17-23; 54:1-6; 60:1-5; 47:1-15).

4. He uses a full, rich vocabulary, but his writing is not artificial or stiff.

5. He uses many beautiful illustrations (see for example, 5:1-7; 12:3; 28:23-29; 32:2).

6. He is versatile in his methods of expression, and is worthy of high praise not only as a writer, but also as an orator and as a poet.

7. His writing is marked by its grandeur and beauty.

8. His diction and choice of words is excellent.

9. His sentences are compact and forceful.

10. He presents a subject, then raises different aspects of the subject as subdivisions.

11. He is able to adapt his language to the occasion.

12. He has noble thoughts and can express them in beautiful and appropriate language.

13. Isaiah makes abrupt jumps and transitions from one period of prophetic fulfillment to another, making it difficult to identify the period about which he is speaking in every instance.

Date of Authorship and Author's Background

c. 700 B.C.

Most critics assert that the book of Isaiah was written by either two or three individuals. The critics are nearly united, at least, in conceding that Isaiah was the author of the first section of the book (chapters 1-39) and that the book was written near the end of his ministry, following Sennacherib's invasion. There is less unity among the critics concerning the existence and time of "second" or "Deutero-Isaiah" and upon the possibility of the existence of a "third" or "Trito-Isaiah."

The problem of the authorship of the book of Isaiah is of major importance to Latter-day Saints because it calls in question the divine origin of the Book of Mormon. The Book of Mormon quotes numerous passages from Isaiah which were found within the brass plates brought to the Americas by Lehi about 600 B.C. Many of the passages it quotes are from the passages the Bible scholars assign to the second and third Isaiahs which, according to their theories, were written long after 600 B.C.

If the theories of the Bible scholars are correct, then the Book of Mormon could not be quoting from the brass plates, and it is a false, or forged book of scripture. On the other hand, if the Book of Mormon is true, then it disproves the theories of the Bible scholars and invalidates the conclusions they have reached on many of the Old Testament books as a result of these same theories. The following information summarizes the matter which is often called the "literary problem of Isaiah" among the Latter-day Saints.

Notes On the Literary Problem of Isaiah and Its Importance For Latter-day Saints

1. **What is the literary problem of Isaiah?**

Bible scholars (higher critics) during the past 180 years have begun to teach that much of the book of Isaiah was not written by that prophet, but rather that it was written by several men who lived several hundred years later. Each scholar has a sightly different arrangement, but in general the scholars break down the book into three sections:

    A. Isaiah: Chapters 1-39.
    B. Deutero-Isaiah (Second Isaiah): Chapters 40-55.
    C. Trito-Isaiah (Third Isaiah): Chapters 56-66.

The higher critics say that Deutero-Isaiah and Trito-Isaiah must have lived much later than the time of Isaiah (740-697 B.C.), at least after the time of Cyrus the Persian (540 B.C.).

2. **What are the major assumptions the higher critics make in studying the prophets?**

The three major assumptions made by the higher critics are:

    A. A prophet speaks only to the people of his own generation, and only about his own time.

B. A prophet speaks out of his own circumstances, and not out of future circumstances.

C. A prophet may anticipate future events only as the current events of his day indicate the future events are to come about.

These assumptions, which are obviously contradictory to the Latter-day Saint concepts of prophecy and revelation, have formed the basis for a major portion of the scholarly criticism of Isaiah. By accepting these assumptions as fact, Bible critics have rejected the possibility of all the far-ranging prophecies of Isaiah having been made by only one man. According to their theories, a prophet can only speak about one period of prophetic fulfillment—not four, as Isaiah does. Their theories have become so strongly entrenched in modern scholarship that they are often presented as fact in modern textbooks.

3. **What other items of evidence do higher critics cite to demonstrate that the book of Isaiah had more than one author?**

A. The *literary style* of Second and Third Isaiah is supposedly different from the part attributed to Isaiah. They say that certain images and phrases are common in the first portion of the book, but that they disappear in the latter portion and are replaced by entirely new images.

B. The *theological ideas* of the latter portion of the book are different than the ideas expressed in the early portion, according to the higher critics. They say, for instance, that the early chapters stress the man-like qualities of God, while the latter chapters stress His majesty and infinitude. Not only the theology of the sections attributed to Deutero-Isaiah and Trito-Isaiah is challenged, however, but also certain teachings in the early portion of the book. Some theological ideas used by Isaiah which the higher critics say were not accepted until much later are:

1. The conversion of the heathen. (2:2-4)
2. The picture of universal peace. (11:1-9)
3. Universal judgment upon the whole earth. (14:26)
4. The apocalyptic character of chapters 24-27 are said to represent a phase of Hebrew thought found only after Ezekiel.
5. The return from captivity. (11:11-16)
6. Prophecies concerning the coming of the Messiah.

4. **Many great scholars through the years have held that the Book of Isaiah is a unity, and have shown that the "critical" hypothesis is far from being proved. What evidence do they cite?**

A. The Jewish and Christian Churches have until the last one hundred and fifty years unhesitatingly assigned the whole book to Isaiah.

B. The Septuagint and other ancient versions of scripture give absolutely no hint of the multiple authorship of Isaiah. The critics have even asserted that ten or more prophets contributed to Isaiah's book. Those who doubt those critics question why the names of all these prophets have been forgotten when they lived much closer to the time of the collector than did Isaiah.

C. Christ and His Apostles assigned the book to Isaiah. The New Testament quotes from thirty-two chapters of Isaiah. Many of these chapters are quoted several times. Fourteen chapters are from chapters 1-25; eighteen chapters are from chapters 40-66.

D. Early historians such as Jesus Ben-Sirach (c. 180 B.C.) and Josephus accepted Isaiah as being the author.

The above are external evidences. Those which follow are internal evidences:

E. Isaiah keeps his personality detached from his prophecies. This is characteristic of both the early and later portion of the book.

F. Every chapter in the book is characterized by the majestic imagery in which the writer revels—the poetic elevation of style and the love of nature.

G. Throughout the book there is the common tendency to repetition.

H. Throughout the book the prophet tends to quote his own words. This habit is more common to Isaiah than to any other prophet. (See for example, 11:6-9; 65:25.)

I. Throughout the book there is an abundant use of alliteration (the repetition of the same sound). This can only be seen, of course, in the Hebrew.

J. Throughout the book many expressions peculiar to Isaiah are repeated, such as "the Holy One of Israel," "the God of Jacob," "the Mouth of the Lord hath spoken it," "Set up an ensign," etc.

K. Throughout the book Isaiah "piles up" ideas or imagery. (See for example, 2:10-17; 65:13-14.)

5. What is the Latter-day Saint attitude concerning the Isaiah problem, and why?

Latter-day Saints believe that the entire book of Isaiah was written by Isaiah and that the book was written during his lifetime. They deny that the latter portion was written after the time of Cyrus the Persian.

Their reason for this belief lies in the Book of Mormon. According to the Book of Mormon account, Lehi and his family obtained the brass plates of Laban about 600 B.C. and left Palestine at that time, yet the Book of Mormon quotes extensively from the sections the higher critics assign to Deutero-Isaiah and Trito-Isaiah and which, they say, were written after Cyrus's time (540 B.C.). The Book of Mormon quotes from the following chapters of Isaiah:[1]

2-14	2 Nephi 12-24
29	2 Nephi 27
48-49	1 Nephi 20-21
50-51	2 Nephi 7-8
52	3 Nephi 20; Mosiah 15:8-10
53	Mosiah 14
54	3 Nephi 22
55	2 Nephi 26:25

6. How have critics of the Book of Mormon tried to use the Isaiah problem against the Church?

They have accepted the multiple-author hypothesis as a fact, and then they have insisted that Deutero-Isaiah and Trito-Isaiah lived after the time that Lehi was to have left Jerusalem. This has been their basis for claiming that the Isaiah passages in the Book of Mormon were merely copied from the King James Version by Joseph Smith. They point out that the Isaiah passages in the Book of Mormon are in "King James English."

The Church answers this charge by pointing out that of the 433 Isaiah verses in the Book of Mormon, 234 of them differ from the King James Version. When the gold plates agreed in thought with the King James Version, Joseph Smith used that version, but where there was disagreement, he made the necessary changes in accordance with the Book of Mormon plates.

------

[1]. The items listed are major quotations. Minor references and allusions are not shown.

Textual Transmission

Most critics regard the text of Isaiah as having been poorly transmitted. Some parts are regarded as being textually corrupt, others as being fragmentary, and still others as being amended and altered by later editorials.

O LORD, thou art my God; I will exalt thee, I will praise thy name; for thou hast done wonderful things; thy counsels of old are faithfulness and truth.

For thou hast been a strength to the poor, a strength to the needy in his distress, a refuge from the storm, a shadow from the heat, when the blast of the terrible ones is as a storm against the wall.

And in this mountain shall the LORD of hosts make unto all people a feast of fat things, a feast of wines on the lees, of fat things full of marrow, of wines on the lees well refined.

And it shall be said in that day, Lo, this is our God; we have waited for him, and he will save us: this is the LORD; we have waited for him, we will be glad and rejoice in his salvation.

(Isaiah 25:1, 4, 6, 9)

3

HISTORICAL SUMMARY: ASSYRIA AND THE FALL OF ISRAEL

Kings of Assyria

The ancient empire of Assyria began to rise from an extended period of decline about the same time that Judah and Israel were divided into separate nations. By Jonah's day it had been a predominant world power for almost a century. Assyria continued to rise in power and dominion, and reached the peak of its control over neighboring territories in the same era as it conquered the kingdom of Israel. A struggle for power between the two sons of Esarhaddon, however, so weakened the empire that it collapsed half a century after reaching its highest glory. Its activity is reflected in the following outline with particular emphasis on its relationship to Israel and Judah.

Previous Kings of the Late Assyrian Empire

(First phase—late kingdom)

Adad-nirari II	c. 911-891 B.C.
Tukulti-Ninurta II	c. 890-884 B.C.
Ashur-nasirpal II	c. 883-859 B.C.
Shalmaneser III	c. 858-824 B.C.
Shamshi-Adad V	c. 823-811 B.C.

1. Adad-nirari III—c. 810-783 B.C.

A. For four years was under the control of the queen-regent Sammuramat.

B. After he was freed from his mother's control he began a great program of conquest, which brought many States, including Syria and Israel (but not Judah) into vassal status. He also conquered Babylonia and Media (as far as the Caspian Sea).

C. Something apparently interrupted the advance of Assyrian arms in the middle of his reign. All his recorded victories of consequence took place in the first half of his reign. From 797 B.C. his records tell virtually nothing of any further exploits.

D. His reign is the period of the prophet Jonah. Some believe that it was Jonah's mission which changed the policies of Adad-nirari III.

2. Shalmaneser IV
c. 783-771 B.C.
3. Assur-Dayan III
c. 771-753 B.C.
4. Asshur-Lush
c. 753-745 B.C.

Under these three kings no policy of aggression was persued. Their laxity allowed many vassal states to throw off Assyrian domination. Revolts took place in Assyria and abroad, and Assyria suffered a rapid decline in prestige.

(Second phase—late kingdom)

5. Tiglath-Pileser III—c. 745-727 B.C. Also known as *Pul*.

A. Brought to the throne by a rebellion in the city of Calah.

B. Probably not of royal blood, for later kings were hostile to his memory.

C. A ruler of extraordinary ability, he restored Assyrian prestige and founded the last and greatest phase of the Assyrian Empire.

D. Resubjugated vassals in Babylonia and western Media.

E. In 743 B.C. he fought a decisive battle with Sarduris of Urartu (Armenia) and began the reconquest of Syria. Uzziah of Judah apparently masterminded the resistance but died during the campaign.

F. He overran the northern area of Israel in 734 B.C. (during the reign of Pekah of Israel) and conquered Damascus, capital of Syria, two years later.

G. He began the Assyrian policy of moving conquered populations to other areas.

6. Shalmaneser V—c. 726-722 B.C.

A. Son of Tiglath-Pileser III.

B. Laid siege to Samaria, capital of Israel, during the reign of Israel's king Hoshea, but died before Samaria fell.

7. Sargon II—c. 721-705 B.C.

    A. An Assyrian army general.

    B. In 721 B.C. he completed the siege of Samaria and deported the ten tribes of Israel to the northern and eastern provinces of the Assyrian Empire.

    C. He defeated the remaining major states of Syria in 720 and 717 B.C.

    D. The major campaign of his career was his invasion, in 714 B.C., of Urartu (Armenia) and the conquest of that nation.

    E. He was troubled by the activities of a Babylonian prince, Merodach-baladan, who made an alliance with Hezekiah, king of Judah, against Assyria. (2 Ki. 20:12; 2 Chron. 32:31; Is. 39:1)

    F. He moved the capital of Assyria from Calah to a new site called Dur-Sharrukin (Khorsabad). Excavations here have been of great value to the history of civilization because archaeological artifacts can be dated to his reign.

8. Sennacherib—c. 704-681 B.C.

    A. Son of Sargon II.

    B. Troubled by many rebellions throughout his rule.

    C. In 701 B.C. he invaded the west and exacted heavy tribute from Hezekiah, king of Judah.

    D. In 698 B.C., apparently because he was defeated by the Babylonians and Elamites in the battle of Khalule, new rebellions broke out. Hezekiah, king of Judah, rebelled and Sennacherib attacked Judah. His army was suddenly smitten (by plague?) and he was compelled to retire to his own territory.

9-10. Sennacherib's two sons—c. 681 B.C.

    A. They assassinated their father but were immediately driven into exile in Armenia by their brother, Esarhaddon.

11. Esarhaddon—c. 681-669 B.C.

    A. One of the greatest kings of Assyria.

    B. He rebuilt Babylon, made it one of his chief capitals, and consolidated Assyrian control of Babylonia.

    C. He invaded Egypt and conquered Memphis.

    D. He repelled the Cimmerians and Scythians near the Caucasus Mountains and, though Assyria lost much territory, saved Assyria from what could have been a disastrous barbarian invasion.

12. Ashurbanipal—c. 668-633 B.C.
  A. Son of Esarhaddon.
  B. The last great king of Assyria.
  C. Completed his father's conquest of Egypt.
  D. Defeated the forces of his brother, Shamashshum-ukin, who had become king of Babylon (Esarhaddon had divided the kingdom between his two sons). The four-year war greatly weakened the Assyrian empire.
  E. Rebellions broke out once again and Assyria crushed Elam and the Arabs. (The collapse of Elam opened the way for the new Aryan state of Persia, which rose to world power by conquering Babylonia in 539 B.C.)
  F. Ashurbanipal was very much interested in scholarship and culture. He had his scholars collect rare tablets and records from throughout the kingdom. To his scholarly interest the world is much indebted for its present-day knowledge of Assyrian and Babylonian literature, history, and higher culture.

The Rapid Decline of Assyria Through a Struggle for Power by the Successors to the Throne—633-606 B.C.

Nabopolassar, a general in the Assyrian army and Chaldean governor of Babylonia, declared his independence and entered into an alliance with the Median king *Cyaxares*, and the Medes and Babylonians rapidly devastated the Assyrian armies.

Three final battles:
  1. The Medes destroyed the ancient capital of Asshur in 614 B.C.
  2. The Medes destroyed Nineveh in 612 B.C.
  3. The Medes destroyed the emergency capital of Haran in 608-606 B.C. and the Assyrian empire collapsed completely.

Kings of Israel (the Northern Kingdom)

The divided kingdom of Israel had nineteen kings. Most of these were wicked men who brought about a rapid decline in the moral integrity of their nation and led their country to a rapid collapse. In the following outline, details of the lives of the kings are included only for those kings who lived during and after the ministry of Elijah.

Early Kings

1. Jeroboam	c. 953-927 B.C.
2. Nadab	c. 927-925 B.C.
3. Baasha	c. 925-901 B.C.
4. Elah	c. 901-899 B.C.
5. Zimri	c. 899-882 B.C.
6. Omri	c. 897-875 B.C.

Kings During the Ministries of Elijah and Elisha

7. Ahab—c. 875-853 B.C. (1 Ki. 16:29-17:1; 18:1-19:2; 20:1-22:40; 2 Chron. 18:33-34)

    A. Son of Omri, captain of the hosts.

    B. He was the most wicked of all the kings of Israel.

    C. He married Jezebel, daughter of Ethbaal, King of the Zidonians. They both became Baal worshippers.

    D. He attempted to kill the prophets of Jehovah.

    E. He was guided by the Lord in twice defeating Benhadad (Ben-ha'-dad) and the Syrian army which had surrounded Samaria. It was prophesied that he would die for releasing Benhadad.

    F. He coveted Naboth's vineyard. Jezebel arranged Naboth's death. Elijah prophesied an end to Ahab's house in the days of his sons.

    G. He made an alliance with Syria against Assyria. They were defeated by Shalmaneser III.

    H. He imprisoned the prophet Micaiah.

    I. Ahab was killed in the battle of Ramoth-gilead, where he was allied with Judah against Syria.

8. Ahaziah—c. 853-851 B.C. (1 Ki. 22:40, 49; 2 Ki. 1:2-17, 2 Chron. 20:35-37)

    A. Son of Ahab.

    B. Conducted a joint maritime venture with Jehoshaphat, king of Judah, which was unsuccessful.

    C. He fell through a lattice and was injured. Elijah promised him he would die.

9. Jehoram—c. 851-843 B.C. (2 Ki. 1:17; 3:1-27; 5:7; 6:8-10, 21-23; 8:16, 25, 28-29; 9:14-26, 29; 2 Chron. 22:5-8)

    A. Son of Ahab. (Ahaziah had no son.)

    B. Also known as *Joram*.

C. He did evil, but he put away the image of Baal his father had made.

D. Moab rebelled against Israel. Israel and Judah won with the help of Elisha.

E. He was wounded by the Syrians under Hazael in the battle of Ramoth-gilead.

F. Killed by Jehu.

10. Jehu—c. 843-815 B.C. (1 Ki. 19:16-17; 2 Ki. 9, 10; 2 Chron. 22:6-9, 25:17)

A. Son of Jehoshaphat, the son of Nimshi.

B. He was anointed by a prophet at Ramoth-gilead and told to smite the house of Ahab. The army accepted him as king.

C. He killed Joram, king of Israel; Ahaziah, king of Judah, and Jezebel.

D. He forced the people of Israel to slay the seventy sons of Ahab.

E. He slew forty-two of the brethren of Ahaziah, former king of Judah.

F. He slew all the worshippers of Baal in Israel.

G. The Lord promised him that his children would occupy the throne of Israel unto the fourth generation.

H. He took no heed to walk in the law of the Lord with all his heart.

I. Hazael, king of Syria, began to attack Israel all along its frontiers.

J. He ruled 28 years.

11. Jehoahaz—c. 815-798 B.C. (2 Ki. 10:35; 13:1-9, 25; 14:1, 8, 17)

A. Son of Jehu.

B. He reigned 17 years.

C. He was an evil king.

D. Syria continually harassed Israel during his reign.

E. Most of his army was smitten by Syria.

12. Joash—c. 798-790 B.C. (2 Ki. 13:10-13, 25; 14:8-16; 2 Chron. 25:17-25)

A. Son of Jehoahaz.

B. Also known as *Jehoash*.

C. He reigned 16 years.

D. He was an evil king.

E. On three occasions he defeated Benhadad of Syria and recovered the cities which his father had lost.

F. He overcame Amaziah and the army of Judah, and broke down a portion of the wall of Jerusalem.

Kings of Israel During the Ministries of Jonah, Amos, Hosea, Micah, and Isaiah

13. Jeroboam II—c. 790-749 B.C. (2 Ki. 13:13; 14:16, 23, 27-29; 15:1, 8)
A. Son of Joash (also known as Jehoash), of the dynasty of Jehu.
B. He reigned 41 years.
C. He was the ablest of the kings of Israel, and the most successful in war.
D. He conquered Damascus and Hamath.
E. His reign enjoyed great prosperity.

14. Zachariah—c. 749 B.C. (2 Ki. 14:29; 15:8-12; 18:2)
A. Son of Jeroboam II.
B. An evil king.
C. Reigned six months.
D. Slain by Shallum.

15. Shallum—c. 749-748 B.C. (2 Ki. 15:10, 13-15)
A. Son of Jabesh. He killed Zachariah to become king.
B. An evil king.
C. Reigned one month.
D. Slain by Menahem.

16. Menahem—c. 748-737 B.C. (2 Ki. 15:14-20)
A. Son of Gadi.
B. He reigned for 10 years.
C. An evil king: he was unspeakably cruel.
D. Kept Pul (Tiglath-Pileser), king of Assyria, from conquering Israel by paying a tribute of 1,000 talents of silver.

17. Pekahiah—c. 737-735 B.C. (2 Ki. 15:22-26)
A. Son of Menahem.
B. He reigned for 2 years.
C. An evil king.
D. Slain by Pekah, son of Remaliah (Pekahiah's captain).

18. Pekah—c. 735-733 B.C. (2 Ki. 15:25-32, 37; 16:1, 5; 2 Chron. 28:6; Is. 7:1)

    A. An evil king.

    B. During his reign Tiglath-Pileser III, king of Assyria, attacked Israel and carried the northern section (Galilee and above) into captivity.

    C. He allied with Rezin, king of Syria, and they together attacked Judah in an effort to force Judah to ally itself with them against Assyria.

    D. Slain by Hoshea.

    E. There is much difficulty in determining the chronology of Pekah's reign.

19. Hoshea—c. 733-722 B.C. (2 Ki. 15:30; 17:1-6; 18:1-10)

    A. Son of Elah.

    B. Paid tribute and served as a puppet king under Shalmaneser V, king of Assyria.

    C. Tried to form an alliance with Egypt to throw off Assyria.

    D. Assyria learned of Hoshea's alliance with Egypt and put him in prison.

    E. Israel fell captive to Assyria after a three-year siege. The siege was begun by the Assyrian king, Shalmaneser V, who died during the siege. The conquest was completed by the Assyrian general, Sargon II, who ascended to the throne of Assyria.

Kings of Judah (the Southern Kingdom)

Judah was ruled by a total of twenty-one kings (including Gedeliah, a provisional governor). Thirteen of these kings are considered in this chapter. Six of the kings ruled during the era of Elijah and Elisha. Four kings ministered to Judah during the missions of Jonah, Amos, Hosea, Micah, and Isaiah.

Early Kings:

1. Rehoboam	c. 953-932 B.C.
2. Abijah	c. 932-929 B.C.
3. Asa	c. 929-873 B.C.

Kings During the Ministries of Elijah and Elisha

4. Jehoshaphat—c. 873-848 B.C. (1 Ki. 15:24; 22; 2 Ki. 1:17; 3:1, 14; 8:16; 12:18; 1 Chron. 3:10; 2 Chron. 17:1-12; 18; 19; 20; 21:1, 2, 12; 22:9)

    A. Son of Asa.

    B. He fortified and strengthened the cities of Judah.

    C. He removed the pagan high places from Judah.

    D. The land was prosperous and at peace during much of his reign.

    E. He united with Ahab, king of Israel, against Syria, to recapture Ramoth-gilead. Ahab was mortally wounded in the battle.

    F. He was a righteous king.

    G. He entered into an unsuccessful sailing venture with Ahaziah, king of Israel.

    H. During his reign Judah was attacked by the Ammonites, Edomites, and Moabites. Judah was saved when the invaders fought among themselves.

5. Jehoram—c. 848-840 B.C. (1 Ki. 22:50; 2 Ki. 8:16-24; 12:18; 1 Chron. 3:11; 2 Chron. 21; 22:1, 6, 11)

    A. Son of Jehoshaphat.

    B. He killed his brothers and the princes of Israel.

    C. He married the daughter of Ahab, king of Israel.

    D. He was an evil king.

    E. Edom rebelled from being ruled by Judah.

    F. Libnah also rebelled.

    G. He built high places and compelled Judah to worship there.

    H. During his reign the Philistines and Arabians sacked Jerusalem.

    I. In fulfillment of prophecy, he died of a terrible disease.

6. Ahaziah—c. 844-843 B.C. (2 Ki. 8:25-29; 9:16-29; 10:13; 12:18; 1 Chron. 3:11; 2 Chron. 22:1-11;) Called *Azariah* (2 Chron. 22:6) and *Jehoahaz* (2 Chron. 21:17).

    A. Son of Jehoram and Athaliah, the daughter of Ahab, king of Israel.

    B. He was an evil king.

    C. He allied with Israel and fought against Syria at Ramoth-gilead.

    D. He visited Jehoram, king of Israel, who was recovering from a wound incurred while fighting against the Syrians.

E. He was slain by Jehu.

F. His mother attempted to destroy all his children, but Joash escaped and was hidden for six years.

7. Athaliah—c. 843-837 B.C. (2 Ki. 8:18, 26-27; 11:1-3, 13-20; 2 Chron. 18:1; 21:6; 22:2, 10-12; 23:12-21; 24:7; 1 Chron. 8:26; Ezra 8:7)

A. Daughter of Ahab, king of Israel.

B. She was the mother of Ahaziah.

C. When Ahaziah was killed, she attempted to kill all his children so she could rule. His son, Joash, escaped.

D. After six years Joash was acclaimed as king and she was slain.

8. Joash—c. 837-797 B.C. (2 Ki. 11, 12, 14:1)

A. Son of Ahaziah.

B. Saved from Athaliah's attempt to murder him by his aunt.

C. Hidden for six years.

D. Established on the throne by Jehoiada the priest.

E. Also called *Jehoash*.

F. He had the house of the Lord repaired.

G. He paid tribute to Hazael, king of Syria.

H. He was killed by his servants after reigning forty years.

9. Amaziah—c. 797-792 B.G. (2 Ki. 12:21; 13:12; 14:1-23; 15:1, 3; 1 Chron. 3:12; 2 Chron. 24:27-26:4)

A. Son of Joash.

B. He slew the servants who had killed his father.

C. He conquered Edom, but brought their gods home and worshiped them.

D. He challenged Jehoash, king of Israel, to war. Israel defeated Judah and plundered Jerusalem.

E. He was murdered in Lachish.

Kings of Judah during the Ministries of Jonah, Amos, Hosea, Micah, and Isaiah

10. Uzziah—c. 792-740 B.C. (2 Ki. 14:21-22; 15:5; 2 Chron. 26:1-23; Zech. 14:5; Is. 6:1)

A. Son of Amaziah.

B. Also called *Azariah* (2 Ki. 14:21) and *Azias* (Mt. 1:8).

C. Built Elath and restored it to Judah.

D. Defeated the Philistines and Arabians.

E. Fortified Jerusalem and maintained a strong army.

F. A good and righteous king. Increased Judah's agricultural capacities.

G. Smitten with leprosy when he tried to usurp priestly authority.

H. Earthquake in his reign.

11. Jotham—c. 749-734 B.C. (2 Ki. 15:5, 32-38; 2 Chron. 27; Is. 1:1, 7:1; Hos. 1:1; Mic. 1:1)

A. Son of Uzziah.

B. A good and righteous king. During much of his reign he was co-regent with Uzziah.

C. Built cities and fortifications.

D. Defeated the Ammonites.

12. Ahaz—c. 734-728 B.C. (2 Ki. 16; 2 Chron. 28; Is. 7)

A. Son of Jotham.

B. An evil king. He turned to idol worship.

C. His kingdom was defeated by Pekah (of Israel) and Rezin (of Syria), but the captors were prevented from keeping their hostages by the prophet Oded.

D. He was told by Isaiah not to fear Israel and Syria.

E. Formed an alliance with Assyria against Israel and Syria while the latter were attacking him.

F. Was forced to pay tribute to Tiglath-Pileser III of Assyria to keep Assyria from conquering Judah.

G. Copied heathen altars and worship forms.

13. Hezekiah—c. 728-697 B.C. (2 Ki. 18-21; 2 Chron. 29-33; Is. 36-38)

A. Son of Ahaz.

B. A righteous king who was a great religious and political reformer.

C. Fought against the idolatry his father had introduced.

D. Defeated the Philistines.

E. The first part of his reign was prosperous.

F. Refused to pay tribute to Assyria.

G. During his reign Israel fell to the Assyrians under Sargon II.

H. The Assyrians under Sennacherib attacked Judah along with other nearby Mediterranean states. Hezekiah was compelled to pay heavy tribute. (701 B.C.)

    I. Through prayer he gained a 15-year extension to his life. (Is. 38)

    J. Hezekiah and Judah again rebelled against Sennacherib and Assyria in 698 B.C.

    K. Assyria attacked Judah and demanded complete surrender. Jerusalem was miraculously saved when 185,000 Assyrians died in one night in fulfillment of a prophecy of Isaiah. (2 Ki. 18-19, Is. 37-38)

Summary

While studying the period of the decline and fall of Israel, the student should know:

Assyria

1. The three most important kings of Assyria were:

    A. *Tiglath-Pileser III*—carried away northern Israel into captivity.

    B. *Sargon II*—captured Samaria and carried the rest of Israel into captivity.

    C. *Sennacherib*—invaded Judah but lost 185,000 men.

Israel

2. The divided kingdom of Israel had nineteen kings, most of whom were wicked.

3. Israel's most important kings were:

    A. *Ahab*—the most wicked; opposed by Elijah.

    B. *Jeroboam II*—extended the boundaries and prosperity of Israel to its greatest extent.

    C. *Pekah*—fought in the Syro-Ephraimite war against Judah; northern Israel went into captivity during his reign.

    D. *Hoshea*—Israel's last king. Israel went into captivity to end his reign.

Judah

4. The kingdom of Judah had twenty-one kings, most of whom were wicked.

5. Judah's most important kings of this period were:

    A. *Jehoshaphat*—a righteous king who was aided by the Lord.

B. *Ahaz*—a wicked king; his alliance with Assyria brought about the fall of Israel.

C. *Hezekiah*—his life was extended 15 years because of righteousness; Sennacherib lost his 185,000 men during his reign.

Important Dates

6. c. 734 B.C.—the Syro-Ephraimite War.[1]

7. c. 734 B.C.—Fall of northern Israel (the Galilee captivity).

8. c. 722 B.C.—Fall of Samaria.

9. c. 698 B.C.—The Lord defeats Sennacherib outside of Jerusalem.

Wash you, make you clean; put away the evil of your doings from before mine eyes; cease to do evil;

Learn to do well; seek judgment, relieve the oppressed, judge the fatherless, plead for the widow.

Come now, and let us reason together, saith the LORD: though your sins be as scarlet, they shall be as white as snow; though they be red like crimson, they shall be as wool.

If ye be willing and obedient, ye shall eat the good of the land:

But if ye refuse and rebel, ye shall be devoured with the sword: for the mouth of the LORD hath spoken it.

(Isaiah 1:16-20)

---

[1] Discussed in Chapter four.

Part II

CHAPTER ANALYSES

For unto us a child is born, unto us a son is given: and the government shall be upon his shoulder: and his name shall be called Wonderful, Counsellor, The mighty God, The everlasting Father, The Prince of Peace.

Of the increase of his government and peace there shall be no end, upon the throne of David, and upon his kingdom, to order it, and to establish it with judgment and with justice from henceforth even for ever. The zeal of the LORD of hosts will perform this.

(Isaiah 9:6-7)

And it shall come to pass in that day, that the remnant of Israel, and such as are escaped of the house of Jacob, shall no more again stay upon him that smote them; but shall stay upon the LORD, the Holy One of Israel, in truth.

The remnant shall return, even the remnant of Jacob, unto the mighty GOD.

For though thy people Israel be as the sand of the sea, yet a remnant of them shall return: the consumption decreed shall overflow with righteousness.

For the Lord GOD of hosts shall make a consumption, even determined, in the midst of all the land.

Therefore thus saith the Lord GOD of hosts, O my people that dwellest in Zion, be not afraid of the Assyrian: he shall smite thee with a rod, and shall lift up his staff against thee, after the manner of Egypt.

For yet a very little while, and the indignation shall cease, and mine anger in their destruction.

(Isaiah 10:20-25)

4

Chapters of Isaiah Pertaining to the First Period of Prophetic Fulfillment: THE FALL OF ISRAEL TO ASSYRIA

Section 1

The following chapters of the book of Isaiah will be considered in this section, in this order: 6, 7, 8, 15, 16, 17, 19, 20, 9, 30, 31, 22, 28, 56, 57, 58, 59, 38, 36, and 37. As a guide to the student, each chapter is briefly outlined. It is suggested that they be read in the order given above so that they can be understood as a chronology of Isaiah's life and times.

The Beginning of Isaiah's Ministry (c. 740 B.C.)

Chapter 6—Isaiah's Call to the ministry.
Note: This chapter is quoted in 2 Nephi 16.
1. Isaiah's vision of the Lord in heaven. (1-4)
2. Isaiah's confession of his sins and his cleansing. (5-7)
3. Isaiah's call to the ministry. (8-11)
4. The captivity of Israel is predicted. (12-13)

Note: Verse 13 is difficult. A tenth was to remain and then it would be eaten. Apparently Judah (more or less a tenth of Israel, or one tribe out of twelve) would be left when Israel was taken captive, and then Judah would later be destroyed.

The Syro-Ephraimite War (c. 734 B.C.)

Chapter 7—To Ahaz (King of Judah): Do not fear Israel and Syria. Prophesied Signs of the Future Birth of Christ.

Note: This chapter is quoted in 2 Nephi 17.

    1. Background on the war. (1-2) (See also 2 Ki. 16; 2 Chron. 28.)

Note: In 734 B.C., Rezin, king of Syria, and Pekah, king of Israel, attempted to force Judah to join them in an alliance against Assyria. Judah's king, Ahaz, refused, so Syria and Israel attacked Judah in an attempt to set a new king on the Jewish throne who would be sympathetic to their plan. (Is. 7:6) Although Syria suffered heavy casualties, she also inflicted heavy losses on Judah and carried a "great multitude" of the Jews captive to Damascus. (2 Chron. 28:5) Israel killed one hundred twenty thousand men of Judah, and took two hundred thousand more to Samaria as captives. (2 Chron. 28:6-8) However, the prophet Oded (O´-děd) was there and he, together with four of the important political figures of Israel, convinced the returning Israelite army that the captives should be freed and sent back to Judah. (2 Chron. 28:9-16) While Judah was in this weakened condition it was attacked by the Edomites and Philistines. (2 Chron. 28:17-19) To relieve the pressure, Ahaz appealed to Tiglath-pileser III of Assyria for help. (2 Chron. 28:20, 2 Ki. 16:7) The Assyrian king used his appeal as an excuse to conquer Syria (2 Ki. 16:9) and to carry a portion of Israel into captivity. For his service to Judah, he required Ahaz to pay a heavy tribute to Assyria. (2 Ki. 16:8, 2 Chron. 28:20-21)

    2. Isaiah's message to Ahaz at the beginning of the war:
        A. Don't be afraid of Israel and Syria. (3-6)
        B. Israel and Syria will not be able to depose Ahaz. (7)
        C. Within 65 years Ephraim (Israel) shall be broken so it will no longer be a nation. (8)

Note: The 65 years is believed to cover the period from the first deportation of Israel (734 B.C.) to the settlement of foreigners in the land by Esarhaddon about 670 B.C. (See 2 Ki. 17:24, Ez. 4:2.)

        D. If ye will not believe, surely ye shall not be established. (9)

E. (III[1]) The Lord's sign to Ahaz that these things would happen: the Immanuel prophecy. (10-16)[2]

F. Ahaz's plan for seeking foreign help will reap unforeseen consequences. Judah will become the arena of conflict between Egypt and Assyria, and will be desolated by Assyria. (17-25)

Chapter 8—To Ahaz (continued): Instead of Forming Foreign Alliances, Trust in the Lord.

Note: This chapter is quoted in 2 Nephi 18.

1. Before Isaiah's newborn son (whose symbolic name, Maher-shal-al-hash-baz, means "the spoil speedeth, the prey hasteth") can talk, Assyria will have conquered Damascus (Syria) and Samaria (Israel). (1-4)

Note: Damascus soon fell to Assyria because of Ahaz's request to Assyria for help. (2 Ki. 16:7-9) The Assyrians took the northern portion of Israel into captivity in 734 B.C. (2 Ki. 15:29)

2. Assyria will not only conquer Syria, it will also attack Judah. (5-8)

Note: This was fulfilled thirty-three years later, in 701 B.C., when Sennacherib invaded Judah. (Is. 36, 37)

3. Alliance with foreign powers will bring Judah's downfall. (9-12)

Note: Ahaz's request for help from Assyria resulted in Judah's becoming a vassal state and increased Judah's idolatry, which was the eventual cause of its downfall. (See 2 Ki. 16:7-18.)

4. Instead of forming foreign alliances, trust in the Lord. (13, 14, 17)
5. Those who do not trust in the Lord shall fall and be taken. (14-22)

Burdens on Surrounding Nations

Chapters 15 and 16—The Burdens of Moab.

1. The nation shall be laid waste, and lions will come upon the remnant that escape. (15:1-9)

2. Isaiah advises Moab that it would be wise to send a messenger to Jerusalem and declare allegiance to Judah. (16:1-5)

3. The people of Moab shall mourn; their prayers in the high places shall not prevail. (16:6-13)

---

[1] The Roman numerals I, II, III and IV which are used throughout Chapters 4 through 7 refer to the four periods of prophetic fulfillment. Arabic numerals in square brackets [ ] at the beginning of a paragraph or item refer to one of the fifty events listed in connection with the fourth period of prophetic fulfillment, the last days, in Chapters 7 and 14.
[2] This prophecy is considered in section III, Chapter 6.

4. Moab shall fall within three years. (16:14)

Note: The cities of Moab were sacked by three different Assyrian kings: Tiglath-Pileser III, in 734 B.C.; Sargon (whose army was led by his son, Sennacherib) in 713 B.C.; and Sennacherib, 701 B.C.

Chapter 17—The Burden of Damascus (Syria).

1. Syria will be made desolate. (1-14)

Note: Syria fell to Tiglath-Pileser III of Assyria in c. 734 B.C.

Chapters 19 and 20—The Burden of Egypt.

1. (II) The Egyptians will be given into the hand of a cruel lord and will be set one against another. (19:1-4)

Note: Sargon II defeated the Egyptians at Raphia in 720 B.C., and Sennacherib defeated them at Eltekeh in 701 B.C., but this does not seem to be the actual fulfillment of the prophecy. It was fulfilled by the Assyrian king Esar-Haddon, who conquered Egypt in 671 B.C. He divided it into a number of small vassal states, the governors of which plundered and spoiled their subjects.

2. Those who labor in Egypt will not be able to find work. (19:5-10, 15)

3. (IV) [34] The leaders of Egypt are not wise, but make their people err. (19:11-14)

4. [34, 35, 40] In that day the Lord will heal Egypt and the Egyptians shall know and worship the Lord. (19:16-22)

Note: While many Jews did live in Egypt in the days of the Savior, primarily at Alexandria and Heliopolis, this would not seem to be the fulfillment of the prophecy. Theirs was not a time when—

    A. Judah was a terror unto Egypt. (17)

    B. Egypt swore allegiance to the Lord of hosts. (18)

    C. A savior came and delivered them from oppressors. (20)

    D. Egypt returned to the Lord. (22)

    E. The Lord regarded Egypt, Israel, and Assyria as equal. (24)

    F. Israel stood as the place of inheritance for the Lord's people. (25)

These clues seem to combine as an indication that the fulfillment of the prophecy is yet future.

5. [34] In that day there will be a highway from Egypt to Assyria and Israel will be a blessing in the Lord. (19:23-25)

6. The Lord commanded Isaiah to go naked and barefoot for three years. This was a sign that Egypt and Ethiopia would be led away prisoners by Assyria in the same condition. (20:1-6)

Note: Tartan came to the Philistine city of Ashdod in 711 B.C.

First Invasion of Israel—The Galilee Captivity (c. 734 B.C.)

Chapter 9—To Ahaz (continued): Israel's Imminent Sorrow Is Contrasted with Its Joy at the Birth of Christ.

Note: This chapter is quoted in 2 Nephi 19.

1. (III) The suffering of the Zebulun (Zĕ-bū´-lun) and Naphtali (Năph´-tă-lī) areas of Israel will someday be alleviated by a visit of Christ to that area. (1-2) (See Mt. 4:12-16.)

Note: This area, the Galilee region, was the first to fall before the Assyrians in c. 734 B.C. (2 Ki. 15:29), yet it would have the honor of being the home of the Savior.

2. (III) The birth of Christ will serve to increase the joy and reduce the burden of the people. (3-7)

Note: Isaiah 9:8 to 10:4 is a poem in four strophes, each with the same refrain: "For all this his anger is not turned away, but his hand is stretched out still."

3. The inhabitants of Samaria shall be devoured by their enemies. (8-12)

4. The Lord will cut off the men and leave only the children and widows. (13-17)

5. No man will spare his brother; they shall suffer hunger. (18-21)

Chapters 30 and 31—The Folly of an Alliance With Egypt.

1. Those who attempt to ally Judah with Egypt sin in so doing because they have not sought God's counsel. Egypt will not help Judah. (30:1-7)

2. The strength of Judah is to sit still and be confident. (30:7, 15-17)

3. Judah's sins are listed. (30:8-13)

4. [30-31] The Lord will be gracious unto His people when they dwell in Zion at Jerusalem. He shall make the ground increase. (30:18-24)

5. [35] There shall be water on every high mountain and the light of the sun shall be sevenfold in the day the towers fall and the Lord heals the wound of His people. (30:25-26)

6. [35] The Lord will sift the nations with destruction through devouring fire, scattering, tempest, and hailstones. (30:27-30)

7. The Assyrian shall be beaten down. (30:31-33)

8. The Egyptians are only men; they will not be able to help Judah like God will. (31:1-3)

9. The Lord will defend, deliver, and preserve Jerusalem. Turn ye to him. (31:4-6)

10. The Assyrians shall flee and be discomfited, and fear the ensign of Jerusalem. (31:7-9)

Note: This seems to refer to Sennacherib's invasion in 698 B.C., in which 185,000 of his men died suddenly. He left Judah and did not return. (See Is. 37.)

Chapter 22—A Reproof of Jerusalem for Its Conduct During Sennacherib's Invasion.

1. The city is joyous because the men have not been slain in battle. (1-7)

2. The people had foolishly attempted to fortify Jerusalem (see also 2 Chron. 32:3-5) instead of trusting in God. (8-14)

3. Demote Shebna (Shĕb´-ña) (it would appear that he was an officer of the city of Jerusalem who may have led the people of the city in their foolish defense) and appoint Eliakim (e-lī´-ă-kim) to rule over the people of the city. The latter shall rule well for a while and then his burden shall be removed. (15-25)

Chapter 28—God's Judgment Upon the Rulers of Israel and Judah.

1. The drunken rulers of Ephraim (Israel) will be trodden under feet. (1-4)

2. [35] In that day the Lord will give his people the spirit of judgment and strength in battle. (5-6)

3. The priests and false prophets have erred through wine. They would not hear when God tried to teach them his precepts. (7-13)

4. The rulers of Judah have falsely assumed that they are righteous enough to escape the overflowing scourge, judgment and hell. They will not escape. (14-22)

5. A parable of sowing and reaping: just as the farmer does not thresh various types of grain with the same degree of force, so God will not punish his people beyond what they deserve. (23-29)

The Fall of Israel (c. 722 B.C.)

Chapter 56—The Nations are Summoned to Devour Israel.

1. Blessed is the man who does justice and observes the sabbath. (1-2)

2. Those who keep the sabbaths and take hold of the covenant without polluting them will come into the Lord's holy mountain. (3-7)

3. [41] The Lord which gathers the outcasts of Israel will gather others to him, beside those that are gathered unto him. (8)

4. The nations (depicted as beasts) are summoned to devour Israel because her watchmen (false prophets), wealthy men (dogs), and rulers (shepherds) are ignorant, greedy, and without understanding. (9-12)

Chapter 57—The Only Hope for Israel Is to Trust God.

1. The people have sinned and debased themselves with idol worship and heathen fertility rites. (1-8)

2. The only hope for Israel is to put its trust in God. (9-16)

3. The Lord will heal the wicked person and restore comforts to him. (17-21)

Chapter 58—True Religious Observance is Required.

1. The people observe the outward ordinances but do not observe the true spirit of worship. (1-4)

2. The Lord defines the proper method of fasting. (5-7)

3. If Israel will aid the hungry and afflicted, and observe the Sabbath properly, the Lord will guide her and aid her. (8-14)

Chapter 59—Sin Separates Man From God.

1. God can save Israel, but their sins have separated them from God. (1-2)

2. Israel's sins are listed. (3-8)

3. Israel's confession of guilt. (9-14)

4. The Lord saw man's need for an intercessor and judge and accepted the task. (15-18)

5. [35, 37] When the enemy shall come in like a flood, the Spirit of the Lord shall lift up a standard against him and the Redeemer shall come to Zion. (19-21)

Hezekiah's Life Is Extended

Chapter 38—Hezekiah's Life Is Extended 15 Years.

1. Isaiah tells the ailing Hezekiah that he is about to die. (1)

2. Hezekiah prays to the Lord. (2-3)

3. The Lord sends Isaiah to Hezekiah to say:

    A. God will extend his life 15 years. (4-5)

    B. God will deliver Hezekiah and Jerusalem out of the hands of the Assyrians. (6)

    C. As a sign, the sun will move 10 degrees backward on the sun dial. (7-8)

4. Hezekiah's hymn of thanksgiving. (9-22)

Sennacherib's Invasions of Judah (c. 713 B.C. and 701 B.C.)

Chapters 36 and 37—Sennacherib's Invasion of Judah.

Note: Isaiah 36 and 37 seem to be a blending of the accounts of two invasions under Sennacherib. The first was in 713 B.C., the second in 701 B.C. It would appear that Hezekiah was able to buy off the Assyrians the first time (2 Ki. 18:14-16). This account appears to be primarily an account of the 701 B.C. invasion, yet it is ascribed to the 14th year of Hezekiah's reign (Is. 36:1), which would indicate the earlier invasion. If Hezekiah's 15-year extension of life preceded the invasion of Is. 36-37, then this is the 701 B.C. attack. If it followed the Is. 36-37 invasion, then this is the 713 B.C. incident. It is impossible to determine the matter since the order in the accounts conflict. Bible scholars and historians are not in agreement as to the events of this period. (See 2 Ki. 18:13-19:36; 2 Chron. 32.)

1. The Assyrian king, Sennacherib, attacked the defensed cities of Judah and conquered many of them. (36:1)

2. He sent an ambassador to Jerusalem while he laid siege to the city of Lachish. (2 Chron. 32:9) Rabshakeh (Răb´shă-kēh), the ambassador, confronted Eliakim (E-lī´-ă-kim), the governor of Jerusalem, outside of Jerusalem. (36:2-3) The Assyrian's message was that

    A. Judah has rebelled against Assyria because of an alliance with Egypt. Egypt will not protect Judah. (36: 4-6)

    B. You cannot rely on Jehovah to protect you. He has sent me to destroy Judah (a false claim). (36:7-10)

    C. Give Assyria 2,000 hostages so it won't destroy Jerusalem. (36:8, 16-17)

    D. Hezekiah (king of Judah) will not be able to deliver you. Don't let him deceive you and make you rely on God. (36:13-15)

    E. Jehovah will not be able to save you. No local God has been able to save other nations from Assyria's might. (36:18-20)

3. When Hezekiah heard from Eliakim the message of Rabshakeh, he sent Eliakim to Isaiah for counsel. (36:21-37:5)

4. Isaiah's message:

    A. Do not be afraid of the blasphemous words of the Assyrians. (37:6)

    B. The Assyrians shall hear a rumor and shall return to their own land. (37:7)

5. The Assyrians heard rumors of an Ethiopian attack and left. (37:8-9)

6. The Assyrians sent a threatening letter to Hezekiah. (37:10-14)

7. Hezekiah's prayer for deliverance. (37:15-20)

8. Isaiah sent the Lord's answer to Hezekiah's prayer:

    A. A taunt-song against Sennacherib. (37:22-29)

    B. The king of Assyria will not come into Jerusalem nor attack it. (37:30-35)

9. The angel of the Lord killed 185,000 of the Assyrians during the night so Sennacherib and his army returned to Nineveh, leaving Jerusalem unharmed. (37:36-37)

Note: Herodotus, in his writings two centuries later, speaks of the tradition of an invasion of rats which attacked Sennacherib's army when it reached the delta, bringing with them the plague.

Summary of Isaiah—Section I

After studying Section I of Isaiah the student should know:

1. Isaiah preached at the time of the fall of Israel.

2. He preached at the time of two major crises of Judah:

    A. The Syro-Ephraimite War.

    B. The Assyrian attack under Sennacherib.

3. Isaiah was mainly concerned with two kings of Judah:

    A. Ahaz

    B. Hezekiah

4. The three major messages of Section I of Isaiah were the same as for Micah and Hosea:

    A. God was displeased with the many sins of Israel.

    B. Israel would be punished by being conquered and scattered among the Gentiles.

    C. God will restore Israel to her former home and prominence in the last days.

5. The first period of prophetic fulfillment was before and during the fall of Israel to Assyria, (800-700 B.C.).

6. Twenty of the sixty-six chapters of Isaiah pertain to the first period of prophetic fulfillment.

7. Isaiah prophesied concerning all four periods of prophetic fulfillment.

And the LORD shall cause his glorious voice to be heard, and shall show the lighting down of his arm, with the indignation of his anger, and with the flame of a devouring fire, with scattering, and tempest, and hailstones.

For through the voice of the LORD shall the Assyrian be beaten down, which smote with a rod.

(Isaiah 30:30-31)

5

Chapters of Isaiah Pertaining to the Second Period of Prophetic Fulfillment: THE FALL OF JUDAH, THE BABYLONIAN CAPTIVITY, AND THE RETURN FROM EXILE

Section II

This section of Isaiah is concerned with his prophecies which pertained to the second period of prophetic fulfillment. It deals primarily with the prophecies of Assyria's fall to Babylonia, the fall of Judah to Babylonia, the fall of Babylonia to the Medes and Persians, and the return of the Jews from the Babylonian captivity. The section includes sixteen chapters: 10, 23, 1, 3, 5, 39, 13, 14, 21, 46, 47, 41, 43, 44, 45, and 48. It is suggested that they be read in the above order so that they will follow in the same chronological order as the events of which they speak.

The Fall of Assyria to Babylon and Media (c. 606 B.C.)

Chapter 10—The Eventual Fall of Assyria.

Note: Verses 1-4 are the final verse of a poem of four strophes which all have the same refrain: "For all this his anger is not turned away, but his hand is stretched out still." The poem begins in 9:8.

Note 2: This chapter is quoted in 2 Nephi 20.

　　1. Woe to those who oppress the poor: they shall fall under the slain. (1-4)

　　2. (I) Assyria will tread down the nation of Israel as a tool of God's anger. (5-10)

　　3. The fate of Samaria will eventually come upon Jerusalem. (11)

　　4. Assyria will boast, not knowing that in its conquests the Lord has used it as a tool. God will punish Assyria and bring its downfall. (12-15)

　　5. [34] The light of Israel will be a flame which will devour the land of Assyria. (16-19)

　　6. [30-31] Item 5 will take place in the day that the remnant of Israel (the ten tribes) and those that are escaped of Jacob (the scattered Jews) shall return and shall rely upon the Lord. (20-22)

　　7. [35] The Lord shall make a consumption in the midst of all the land. (23)

　　8. Do not be afraid of Assyria, for the time will come when it will be destroyed, and its yoke will be removed from Judah. (24-34)

Tyre to Be Destroyed

Chapter 23—The Burden of Tyre.
　　1. Tyre shall be desolate and forgotten. (1-12)
　　2. Behold the land of the Chaldeans (Babylonia). (13)
　　3. Tyre will be forgotten for 70 years and then shall be restored. (14-18)

Note: Tyre was conquered by Nebuchadnezzar, king of Babylonia, after a thirteen-year siege (585-573 B.C.). (See also Ezek. 26-28.)

The Fall of Judah to Babylonia

Chapter 1—"The Great Arraignment" of Judah and Jerusalem.

Note: This chapter may best be understood as a court scene, with Jehovah as the judge and Judah as the defendant.

1. The Lord's charge:
    A. Judah has rebelled against me. (2-4)
    B. The land of Judah will be left desolate and only a small remnant shall remain. (5-9)
2. The Lord anticipates and rejects Judah's defense:
    A. Sacrifices, burnt offerings and other outward manifestations of worship are vain before God (because they are a sham which hides evil deeds and minds.) (10-15)
    B. Cease to do evil, learn to do well. (16-17)
3. The Lord offers to pardon Judah:
    A. If ye be willing and obedient, ye shall eat the good of the land. (18-19)
    B. If ye refuse and rebel, ye shall be devoured with the sword. (20)
4. The Lord's sentence of judgment:
    A. The sins of the people are itemized. (21-23, 29)

Note: Verse 29 is seemingly a reference to the groves in which heathen fertility rites were practiced.

    B. The Lord will avenge himself of his enemies, and they that forsake the Lord shall be consumed. (24-25, 28-31)
5. The Lord's judgment will make possible the eventual restoration of Judah:
    A. [35] The Lord will ease Himself of His enemies and will purge the dross of Israel. (24-25)
    B. [41] Afterward thou shalt be called the city of righteousness, the faithful city. Zion shall be redeemed with judgment. (26-27)
    C. [42] The destruction of the transgressors and of the sinners shall be together they shall be burned and consumed. (28-31)

Chapter 3—The Men of Judah to Fall
Note: This chapter is quoted in 2 Nephi 13.

1. The leaders of Judah will be taken away from Jerusalem. (1-3)
2. Judah will be ruled by children and women. (4-8, 12)
3. The wicked people have rewarded evil unto themselves. (9-11)
4. The Lord will punish the ancients ("wise" leaders) and princes of the people for oppressing the poor. (13-15)
5. The Lord will punish the haughty daughters of Zion, for their men shall fall by the sword, and their mighty in the war. (16-26)

6. **Note:** It would seem that verse one of chapter 4 might well be included with chapter 3, as a continuation of the explanation of how the men of Judah will fall and/or be carried away captive:

> Ch. 4:1—And in that day seven women shall take hold of one man, saying, We will eat our own bread, and wear our own apparel: only let us be called by thy name, to take away our reproach.

The question of whether Is. 4:1 belongs with chapter 3 or chapter 4 is an important one. If the verse belongs with the preceding chapter, then it is a prophecy of the suffering of the women of Judah when their men were carried into exile at the time of the fall of Jerusalem to the Babylonians. (See 2 Ki. 24:14-16, 25:8-12; Jer. 52.) There can be little doubt that this situation offered ample fulfillment, if this interpretation of the passage is correct. This seems to be the logical understanding of the passage.

On the other hand, if Is. 4:1 is connected with the thought of Is. 4:2-6, then it is a prophetic indication of a future imbalance of the sexes among God's people either (1) during a period of the establishment of the New Jerusalem in Jackson County, Missouri, or (2) during the era of the latter-day Jerusalem in Palestine. Again the matter rests on the interpretation of Is. Chap. 4.

Chapter 5—The Parable of the Vineyard—God's Judgment Upon Judah.

Note: This chapter is quoted in 2 Nephi 15.

1. The parable:
    A. The well beloved had a vineyard which he gave great care, but it brought forth wild grapes. (1-4)
    B. The Lord will make the vineyard barren. (5-6)
    C. The vineyard of the Lord of hosts is the house of Israel, and the men of Judah his pleasant plant. (7)
2. Six woes upon Judah:
    A. Woe unto them who acquire much property (by oppressing the poor). Many houses shall be desolate. (8-10)
    B. Woe unto them who are drunkards instead of considering the work of the Lord. The people are gone into captivity because they have no knowledge. (11-17)
    C. Woe unto them that mock the Lord and ask that He hasten His work. (18-19)

D. Woe unto them that call evil good and good evil. (20)

E. Woe unto them that are wise in their own eyes. (21)

F. Woe unto them that justify the wicked for reward (take bribes). Their carcasses shall be torn in the midst of the streets. (22-25)

3. The gathering of the house of Israel in the last days:

A. [30-31] God will lift up an ensign to the nations from far, and will hiss unto them from the end of the earth. (26)

Note: See 2 Nephi 29:1-2.

B. [35] Israel shall be powerful and lay hold of the prey. (27-29)

Note: This does not appear to be the same conflict of Micah 5:6-14, 3 Ne. 20:15-20, and 3 Ne. 21:12-21, which the Book of Mormon context shows as taking place in the Americas. This is apparently a reference to the Battle of Armageddon, in which Israel is victorious but sorrows for the loss of two-thirds of its people. (See Zech. 13:7-9.)

C. [35] In that day there will be darkness and sorrow in the land. (30) (See Joel 3:12-15.)

Chapter 39—Judah's Treasures Shall Be Carried Into Babylon.

Note: Review Chapter 38.

1. Merodach-baladan (Mĕr´-ō-dăch-băl´-ă-dăn), the Babylonian prince, sent messengers carrying gifts to Hezekiah to celebrate his recovery from sickness. (1)

2. Hezekiah showed the messengers the treasures of Judah. (2)

3. Isaiah, upon learning what the messengers had seen, prophesied that the treasures of Judah would be carried into Babylon. (3-8)

The Fall of Babylonia to Persia

Chapter 13—The Burden of Babylon.

Note: This chapter is quoted in 2 Nephi 23.

1. God will call his sanctified ones (Cyrus the Persian) and mighty ones (the Medes and the Persians) to defeat the Babylonians. (1-3)

2. The kingdoms of nations will gather together (the Persians will combine with the Medes and other armies they conquered) and come from a far country (Persia) to attack. (4-5)

3. [42] The cruel destruction of Babylon is compared to the destruction at the coming of the Savior. (6-13)

Note: The comparison begins in verse 6: "It shall come **as a destruction from the Almighty."**

　　4. The Medes will be stirred up against Babylon. (17-18)

　　5. Babylon shall be desolate and shall never be inhabited again. (19-22)

Chapter 14—The Fall of Babylon.

Note: This chapter is quoted in 2 Nephi 24.

　　1. Israel will return (from Babylon) to their own land, and strangers shall be joined with them. (1-3)

Note: See the book of Ezra for the fulfillment of this prophecy.

　　2. Israel's taunt-song against Babylon. (4-21)

　　　　A. The Babylonian king is pictured as dying and going to hell, where the other spirits mock him, asking if he is now as weak as they. (9-11)

　　　　B. The fall of the king of Babylon is compared with the fall of Lucifer. (12-15) (See Rev. 12:3, 7-9; D&C 76:25-28; Jn. 8:44.)

　　　　C. The Babylonian king will not even receive proper burial. (16-21)

　　3. The Lord will cut off from Babylon both its name and its posterity. (22-23)

　　4. The Assyrians will also be broken by the Lord. (24-28)

　　5. The burden of Philistia. (29-32)

　　Note: a.　"Philistia" is the name from which "Palestine" is derived.

　　　　b.　The serpent whose rod is broken (29) probably alludes to the death of Tiglath-Pileser III, king of Assyria, who had conquered many Philistine cities.

　　　　c.　The cockatrice and the flying serpent (29): Sargon II and his son, Sennacherib.

　　　　d.　Messengers (32)—probably Philistine ambassadors sent to Jerusalem soliciting help against the Assyrians.

　　　　e.　Other prophecies against the Philistines: Jer. 47, Amos 1:6-8, Zeph. 2:4-7, Zech. 9:5-7.

　　　　A. The Philistines will be slain and dissolved. (29-32)

Chapter 21—The Burden of Babylon, Edom, and Arabia.

Note: a.   Desert of the sea (1)—Babylon. (See v. 9.)

        b.   Elam (2)—Persia.

        c.   Dumah (11)—A district south of Edom, of which Seir was the central area. Here used for Edom.

        d.   Dedanim (13)—Arabic nomads.

1. Babylon will be besieged and spoiled by the Persians and Medes. (1-4) (See Dan. 5:30-31.)

2. The Lord's watchman will report that Babylon is fallen. (5-10)

3. The burden of Edom. (11-12)

4. (I) The burden of Arabia--within a year, all the glory of Kedar shall fail. (13-17)

Note: Sargon II, king of Assyria, invaded Arabia c. 716 B.C.

Chapter 46—The Fall of Babylon.

1. Bel (the chief god of Babylon—See Jer. 50:2) and Nebo (the interpreter of the gods) will not be able to keep Babylon from going into captivity. (1-2)

2. Jehovah, who has supported his followers throughout their lifetime, is greater than the idols. (3-11)

3. The Lord will bring a ravenous bird from the east (Cyrus), who will execute His judgment. (11)

4. [39?] The Lord will place His salvation and glory in Zion. (12-13)

Chapter 47—The Fall of Babylon

1. Babylon will be brought down, for she will show no mercy to the Lord's people. (1-15)

Note: Chapter 47 is a taunt-song of four stanzas: 1-4, 5-7, 8-11, and 12-15.

Judah's Return from the Babylonian Captivity

Chapter 41—Judah's Return from Babylonia.

Note: This chapter is one of the most difficult to interpret of Isaiah's prophecies.

1. Isaiah foresees the rising up of Cyrus the Persian (?). (1-3)

Note: The individual is so identified by most Bible scholars because:

      A. He is from the east (Persia?),

      B. And from the north. This is often interpreted in either of two ways: (1) Cyrus, as head of the Persian armies, had conquered the Median armies and stood as leader of the combined forces; Media is north of Palestine; or (2) Armies from the east always entered Palestine from the north.

     C. He was a righteous man, who ruled over kings. (2)

     D. Although Cyrus is not mentioned by name, the description is similar to Isaiah's description of him in 44:28 and 45:1.

    2. God has chosen Israel and has not cast her away. (4-10)

    3. [35] Those who have warred against Israel shall not be found. (11-14)

    4. [30-31] Israel will thresh the mountains. God will open up rivers in high places and fountains in the valleys so people will know God has helped Israel. (15-20) (cf. Is. 30:25-26.)

    5. The pagan gods are challenged to predict their future activities in advance. Only Jehovah can do so. (21-29)

Chapter 43—The Lord Will Claim His People When Babylon Falls.

    1. The Lord redeemed Israel and will protect her. (1-4)

    2. [30-31] The Lord will gather the seed of Israel from the east, west, north and south. (5-7)

    3. The Israelites are the Lord's witnesses that he is God and the only Savior. (8-13)

    4. The nobles of Babylon shall lie down together and be extinct. (14-17)

    5. [30-31] The Lord will make a way in the wilderness, and rivers in the desert for his chosen people. (18-21)

    6. Though Israel has sinned, the Lord will blot out her transgressions. (22-28)

Chapters 44 and 45—The Lord Will Raise Up Cyrus and Guide Him.

    1. The Lord will bless Israel's crops and offspring. (44:1-5)

    Note: Jesurun means "upright." It is a symbolic name for Israel. (See Deut. 32:15.)

    2. There is no God beside Jehovah. Worship ping idols is meaningless. (44:6-20)

    3. The Lord has redeemed Israel. (44:21-27)

    4. Cyrus (the Persian) will cause Jerusalem to be built. (44:28, 45:13)

    5. The Lord will raise up Cyrus and guide him, though he will not know Him. (45:1-6)

6. Jehovah created the heavens and the earth. He is superior to idols. (45:7-22)

7. [47] The Lord has sworn that every knee shall bow and every tongue shall acknowledge Him. (45:23-25)

Chapter 48—The Lord Will Not Cast Off His People When Babylon Is Destroyed.

Note: This chapter is quoted in 1 Nephi 20. It is regarded as a recapitulation of Isaiah Chapters 40-47.

1. Hear this, you religious hypocrites who swear by the name of the Lord but are not righteous. (1-2)

2. The Lord has declared things from the beginning so when the prophecies came to pass they would know it was His work and not the work of idols. (3-8, 16-17)

3. To maintain His good name, the Lord will not cut off Israel. (9-13)

4. The Lord's arm shall be on Babylon. Go ye forth from there. (14, 20)

5. God provided water for his people as they came through the desert. (21-22)

Summary of Isaiah Section II

After studying Section II of Isaiah the student should know:

1. The second period of prophetic fulfillment was before and during the fall of Judah, the Babylonian captivity and the Jewish return to Palestine (primarily 635-535 B.C.).

2. Sixteen of the sixty-six chapters of Isaiah pertain to the second period of prophetic fulfillment.

3. The four major events of this period of which Isaiah prophesied were:

    A. The fall of Assyria to Babylon and Media.

    B. The fall of Judah to Babylonia.

    C. The fall of Babylonia to Persia.

    D. Judah's return from the Babylonian captivity.

4. One of Isaiah's most profound prophecies was his identification of Cyrus the Persian as the individual who would allow the Jews to return to Palestine.

5. This section contains numerous teachings in three major doctrinal areas:

        A. The nature of sin.
        B. The nature of God.
        C. The nature of revelation.

The burden of Babylon, which Isaiah the son of Amoz did see.

Lift ye up a banner upon the high mountain, exalt the voice unto them, shake the hand, that they may go into the gates of the nobles.

I have commanded my sanctified ones, I have also called my mighty ones for mine anger, even them that rejoice in my highness.

The noise of a multitude in the mountains, like as of a great people; a tumultuous noise of the kingdoms of nations gathered together: the LORD of hosts mustereth the host of the battle.

They come from a far country, from the end of heaven, even the LORD, and the weapons of his indignation, to destroy the whole land.

Howl ye; for the day of the LORD is at hand; it shall come as a destruction from the Almighty.

(Isaiah 13:1-6)

6

Chapters of Isaiah Pertaining to the Third Period of Prophetic Fulfillment THE MINISTRY OF CHRIST IN THE MERIDIAN OF TIME

Most of Isaiah's prophecies concerning the earthly ministry of Christ do not stand as the major subject of his chapters. Rather, they are important insights into the Savior's ministry which are given in contrasting Isaiah's day with that of the Christ. Consequently, the pattern of considering the entire chapter in the context of the period of prophetic fulfillment of its major items will not be completely observed in this section. Instead, commentary on ten chosen passages, plus three chapter outlines (Chapters 42, 50, 53) will be given.

The Birth of the Savior

Isaiah 7:14-16

Therefore the Lord himself shall give you a sign; Behold, a virgin shall conceive, and bear a son, and shall call his name Immanuel.

Butter and honey shall he eat, that he may know to refuse the evil, and choose the good.

For before the child shall know to refuse the evil, and choose the good, the land that thou abhorrest shall be forsaken of both her kings.

Explanation:

1. The entire chapter is outlined in Section I.

2. In the early days of the Syro-Ephraimite war Isaiah prophesied to Ahaz, king of Judah, that Israel and Syria would not be able to conquer Judah. Isaiah offered to show Ahaz a sign from the Lord to show that his prophecy was true, but Ahaz refused to ask for one. Isaiah insisted that a sign be given, saying that the Lord Himself would give it, and then he prophesied of the Lord's birth. His prophecy concerned an event which was to take place more than seven centuries later.

3. This passage was quoted to Joseph, the intended husband of Mary (the mother of Jesus), as evidence that Mary's child-to-be was the result of God's will and that Mary still retained her virginity. (See Mt. 1:18-25)

4. See also Lu. 1:27; 1 Ne. 11:13, 15, 18, 20; 2 Ne. 17:14-16; Al. 7:10.

The Birth of the Savior

Isaiah 9:6-7

For unto us a child is born, unto us a son is given: and the government shall be upon his shoulder: and his name shall be called Wonderful, Counsellor, The mighty God, the everlasting Father, The Prince of Peace.

Of the increase of his government and peace there shall be no end, upon the throne of David, and upon his kingdom, to order it, and to establish it with judgment and with justice [44] from henceforth even for ever. The zeal of the Lord of hosts will perform this.

Explanation:

1. The entire chapter is outlined in Section I.

2. This passage first tells of the birth of the Savior, and then describes the peace and order which will characterize the eternal reign of the Lord and those who rule under His direction on the throne of David in the last days.

The Savior's Labors in Galilee

Isaiah 9:1-2

Nevertheless the dimness shall not be such as was in her vexation, when at the first he lightly afflicted the land of Zebulun and the land of Naphtali, and afterward did more grievously afflict her by the way of the sea, beyond Jordan, in Galilee of the nations.

The people that walked in darkness have seen a great light: they that dwell in the land of the shadow of death, upon them hath the light shined.

Explanation:
1. The entire chapter is outlined in Section I.
2. This prophecy of the Savior, together with the messianic prophecy in Chapter 9, verses 6 and 7, were apparently given by Isaiah as words of comfort for the people taken by Assyria in the Galilean captivity (c. 734 B.C.). He prophesied of Christ's early ministry in their area.
3. Matthew explained the fulfillment of the prophecy:

Now when Jesus had heard that John was cast into prison, he departed into Galilee;

And leaving Nazareth, he came and dwelt in Capernaum, which is upon the sea coast, in the borders of Zabulon and Nephthalim:

That it might be fulfilled which was spoken by Esaias the prophet, saying,

The land of Zabulon, and the land of Nephthalim, by way of the sea, beyond Jordan, Galilee of the Gentiles;

The people which sat in darkness saw great light; and to them which sat in the region and shadow of death light is sprung up. (Mt. 4:12-16)

A Stumbling Block to Israel

Isaiah 8:13-14
Sanctify the Lord of hosts himself; and let him be your fear, and let him be your dread.

And he shall be for a sanctuary; but for a stone of stumbling and for a rock of offense to both the houses of Israel, for a gin and for a snare to the inhabitants of Jerusalem.

Explanation:
1. The entire chapter is outlined in Section I.
2. Jesus truly was a stumbling stone for Judah. They crucified him and have reaped continual persecution for their deed for centuries.

A Sure Foundation Stone

Isaiah 28:16
Therefore thus saith the Lord God, Behold, I lay in Zion for a foundation a stone, a tried stone, a precious corner stone, a sure foundation: he that believeth shall not make haste.

Explanation:

1. The entire chapter is outlined in Section I.

2. Peter explained the passage when he wrote,

Ye also, as lively stones, are built up a spiritual house, an holy priesthood, to offer up spiritual sacrifices, acceptable to God by Jesus Christ.

Wherefore also it is contained in the scripture, Behold, I lay in Sion a chief corner stone, elect, precious: and he that believeth on him shall not be confounded. (1 Pet. 2:5-6)

Preceded by John the Baptist

Isaiah 40:3

The voice of him that crieth in the wilderness, Prepare ye the way of the Lord, make straight in the desert a highway for our God.

Explanation:

1. The entire chapter is outlined in Section IV.

2. The context of this passage clearly shows it to be a prophecy of a forerunner of Christ in the last days (see verses 4 and 5). Latter-day Saints believe this forerunner to be John the Baptist, who restored the Aaronic Priesthood to Joseph Smith on May 15, 1829 (see Mal. 3:1-3 and Mt. 11:10-14; JS-History 1:26-72; D&C 84:27-28; D&C 27:7-8)

3. The New Testament writers, however, regarded John's ministry in their day as being the fulfillment of Isaiah's prophecy:

In those days came John the Baptist, preaching in the wilderness of Judaea,

And saying, Repent ye: for the kingdom of heaven is at hand.

For this is he that was spoken of by the prophet Esaias, saying, The voice of one crying in the wilderness, Prepare ye the way of the Lord, make his paths straight (Mt. 3:1-3. See also Mk. 1:3; Lk. 3:5; Jn. 1:23.)

The First Servant Song—Christ's Characteristics and Deeds

Chapter 42:

Note: Verses 1-9 are the first of four "Servant Songs" in which Isaiah describes the Lord.

1. The Savior's characteristics and deeds are listed:
   - **A. Characteristics**
     - (1). He shall have God's spirit. (1)
     - (2). He shall not cry, nor lift up (boast). (2)
     - (3). He shall be gentle. (3)

(4). He shall not fail nor be discouraged. (4)
(5). He is the Lord. (8)
(6). He will not give his glory to another. (8)
(7). He will not praise graven images. (8)
(8). He will declare new things before they come to pass. (9)

B. Deeds
(1). [4] He shall bring forth judgment to the Gentiles. (1)
(2). [44] He shall set judgment in the earth unto truth. (3-4)
(3). He created the heavens and the earth. (5)
(4). He gives breath and spirit to people. (5)
(5). He will serve as a covenant for the people. (6)
(6). [7] He will be a light unto the Gentiles. (6)
(7). He will heal the blind. (7)
(8). [46] He will bring prisoners from the (spirit ?) prison. (7)

2. A song of praise for God. (10-13)
3. The Lord proclaims the mighty deeds He will do, causing those who have not trusted Him to be ashamed. (14-17)
4. (I) Israel is the Lord's servant, but is blind. (18-22)
5. (I) The Lord has given Israel to the robbers because it sinned against Him. (23-25)

The Second Servant Song—Christ's Characteristics and Deeds
Is. 49:1-13
1. The entire chapter is outlined in Section IV.
2. In this section the Savior seems to be speaking of his mission with scattered Israel. As in the first Servant Song, He lists both His characteristics and His deeds.

A. Characteristics
(1). He was called from the womb. (5)
(2). He was known by name before birth. (1)
(3). His judgment and work is with God. (4)
(4). He is faithful. (7)

B. Deeds
(1). He has made Isaiah his servant so he may be glorified. (2-3)
(2). [30-31] He will raise up the tribes of Jacob. (6)
(3). [30-31] He will restore the preserved of Israel. (6)
(4). [7] He will be a light to the Gentiles. (6)

(5). He is the source of the earth's salvation. (6)

(6). He will be a covenant for the people. (8)

(7). [46] He shall release prisoners. (9)

(8). He will comfort His people. (13)

(9). He will have mercy upon the afflicted. (13)

The Third Servant Song—Christ's Suffering and Passion

Chapter 50

Note: This chapter is quoted in 2 Nephi 8.

1. (I) The Lord has not divorced Israel. You have sold yourselves through sin. (1)

2. The Lord still has power to deliver and redeem His people. (2-3)

3. The Servant Song: The Lord's Suffering and Passion. (4-11)

    A. He gave his back to the smiters. (6) (See Mk. 14:65.)

    B. He hid not his face from shame and spitting. (6) (See Mk. 14:65.)

    C. God will help Him. (7-9)

    D. Trust in the Lord. (10-11)

The Fourth Servant Song—Christ's Suffering and Passion

Chapter 53

Note: The "Servant Song" extends from 52:13 to 53:12. Chapter 53 is quoted in Mosiah 14.

1. He shall grow up as a tender plant, and as a root out of dry ground. (2)

2. He hath no form nor comeliness, nor beauty that he should be desired. (2)

3. He is despised, not esteemed, and rejected of men. (3) (See Jn. 1:11.)

4. He is a man of sorrows, and acquainted with grief. (3)

5. He has borne our griefs and carried our sorrows. (4) (See Mt. 8:16-17.)

6. He was wounded for our transgressions and bruised for our iniquities. (5) (See Rom. 4:25.)

7. With His stripes we are healed. (5) (See 1 Pet. 2:24.)

8. He opened not His mouth. (7) (See Mt. 27:11-14.)

9. He was taken from prison and from judgment. (8) (See Mk. 15:1-15.)

10. He was cut off out of the land of the living. (8)

11. For the transgression of the people was He stricken. (8)

12. He made his grave with the wicked, He was numbered with the transgressors. (9, 12) (See Mt. 27:38.)

13. He was with the rich in his death. (9)

14. He bare the sin of many and made intercession for the transgressors. (10-12) (See Rom. 8:34.)

An Intercessor

Isaiah 59:15-16

Yea, truth faileth; and he that departeth from evil maketh himself a prey: and the Lord saw it, and it displeased him that there was no judgment.

And he saw that there was no man, and wondered that there was no intercessor: therefore his arm brought salvation unto him; and his righteousness, it sustained him.

Explanation:

1. The entire chapter is outlined in Section 1.

2. One function Jesus fulfills is that of making intercession for man with the Father. (See Heb. 7:25; Rom. 8:27.)

Christ Sent to Proclaim the Acceptable Year of the Lord

Isaiah 61:1-2

The Spirit of the Lord God is upon me; because the Lord hath anointed me to preach good tidings unto the meek; he hath sent me to bind up the brokenhearted, to proclaim liberty to the captives, and the opening of the prison to them that are bound;

To proclaim the acceptable year of the Lord, and the day of vengeance of our God; to comfort all that mourn; . . .

Explanation:

1. The entire chapter is outlined in Section IV.

2. Christ, while teaching in the synagogue in Nazareth, read this scripture from "the prophet Esaias" and then told the congregation, "This day is this scripture fulfilled in your ears." (See Lk. 4:16-21.)

The Dead to Rise with Him

Isaiah 26:19

Thy dead men shall live, together with my dead body shall they arise. Awake and sing, ye that dwell in dust: for thy dew is as the dew of herbs, and the earth shall cast out the dead.

Explanation:

1. The entire chapter is outlined in Section IV.

2. Many of the righteous dead were resurrected and came out of their graves at the time Jesus was resurrected. (See Mt. 27:52-53.)

Summary of Isaiah—Section III

After studying Section III of Isaiah the student should know:

1. Isaiah prophesied of many events in the mortal life of the Savior, including:

> A. *His birth*
>
> > —A virgin shall conceive, and bear a son, and shall call his name Immanuel.
> >
> > —For unto us a child is born, unto us a son is given.
>
> B. *His Galilean ministry*
>
> > —The people that dwelt in darkness have seen a great light.
>
> C. *His forerunner*, John the Baptist
>
> > —The voice of him that crieth in the wilderness.
>
> D. *His suffering*
>
> > —He gave his back to the smiters.
> >
> > —He hid not his face from shame and spitting.
>
> E. *His death*
>
> > —He has borne our griefs and carried our sorrows.
> >
> > —He was wounded for our transgressions and bruised for our iniquities.
> >
> > —He bare the sin of many and made intercession for the transgressors.
>
> F. *His resurrection*
>
> > —Thy dead men shall live, together with my dead body shall they arise.

2. Reference to many of Isaiah's prophecies concerning Christ is made in New Testament passages.

3. The third period of prophetic fulfillment deals with events pertaining to the ministry of Christ in the meridian of time.

4. Three of the sixty-six chapters of Isaiah, plus numerous other passages, refer to the third period of prophetic fulfillment.

5. These three chapters are "Servant Songs."

7

Chapters of Isaiah Pertaining to the Fourth Period of Prophetic Fulfillment: THE LAST DAYS

The chapters discussed in this section form the largest portion of the book of Isaiah and pertain to the most predominant theme of the Old Testament prophets. The prophecies of the last days are important to everyone, for in them modern man finds the future laid out in a pattern before him. In them he finds a pattern by which he can prepare for that which lies ahead. This pattern is the plan which God has devised for His children in the last days. These prophecies are subject to interpretation and the interpretation, like the prophecy itself, must be made under inspiration and through the spirit of prophecy.

The vast amount of prophetic material found in the Old Testament creates an almost overwhelming obstacle to the beginning student of prophecy. The material is interrelated and complicated and requires an extensive background for one to be able to fully understand it. To aid the reader in the consideration of the prophecies of the last days, a chronological list of fifty events has been established, [1] and is explained in detail in Chapter 14. Each major prophesied event has been placed in a numbered order.

The entire scope of the eschatological[2] prophecies made by Isaiah which are to be studied in this section is keyed with the number code which refers to these 50 events. The author recognizes that all students will not agree in every instance with his relegation of the prophecies to the predetermined future event. (Wouldn't it be a drab world if everyone did agree on such matters?!) Nevertheless, it is his belief that the number key can serve as a helpful device to aid people in their study of Old Testament prophecies. Section IV of Isaiah is a consideration of twenty-seven chapters: 29, 18, 54, 49, 52, 35, 27, 55, 11, 51, 4, 62, 60, 61, 66, 12, 40, 2, 63, 64, 26, 24, 34, 33, 65, 32, and 25. As in the previous sections on Isaiah, the chapters of this section are arranged in a chronological order according to when they will take place. It will be helpful to read and study them in this order.

Restoration of the Book of Mormon

Chapter 29—The Coming Forth of the Book of Mormon.

Note: This chapter would be one of the most difficult of all the prophecies in the Bible, if it were not for the aid of a passage from the Book of Mormon which clarifies it and gives it the necessary interpretation. In the Book of Mormon passage (2 Nephi chapters 26 and 27) Nephi shows that the prophecy deals with eight items (numbers 2-9 below) which are connected with the Book of Mormon and the restoration of the gospel.

1. *A change of subject.* Verses 1 and 2 begin by talking about Ariel (Jerusalem) and the manner in which it will be distressed. Then the subject is changed with these words: *and it shall be unto me as Ariel* (1-2), and the prophecy speaks of events which were to take place in the Americas.

2. (2) *The fall of the Nephites and the preserving of the Book of Mormon plates.* (3-5)

    A. I will camp against thee round about. (3) *The Nephites were to be surrounded.* (See 2 Ne. 26:15; Morm. 6:1-5, 7-8.)

---

[1] The ordered list has been adapted from the author's books *Prophecy—Key to the Future, Inspired Prophetic Warnings,* and *The Prophecies of Joseph Smith.* Evidence for his ordering of the prophetic events will be found in those volumes, particularly *Prophecy—Key to the Future,* which was a Master's thesis written at Brigham Young University in the College of Religious Instruction, in fulfillment of the assignment to identify and document the chronology of coming last-days events. They also serve to give a fuller and more complete explanation of the prophesied events of the last days than is attempted in this volume.

[2] Means "of, or pertaining to, the last days."

B. Thou shalt be brought down. (4) *The Nephites were to be defeated.* (See 2 Ne. 26:15.)

C. Thou shalt speak out of the ground. (4) *The Nephite records would be preserved and would come forth out of the ground.* (See 2 Ne. 26:16, Morm. 6:6, 14; Moro. 10:2; JS Hist. 1:59.)

D. Thy voice shall be as one that hath a familiar spirit. (4) *Those who heard the message of the Nephite records would recognize it as being something familiar to them.* (See 2 Ne. 26:16, 30:4-6.)

E. It shall be at an instant suddenly. (5) *The battle will be of short duration.* (See 2 Ne. 26:18, Morm. 6:9-15.)

3. Thou shalt be visited with thunder, earthquake, noise. storm, and fire. (6) *The great destruction which came to the Americas at the time of Christ's crucifixion.* (See 3 Ne. 8.)

4. [1] The Lord hath covered your prophets and seers. (9-10) *The apostate condition that befell the Lamanites and the world in general.* (See 2 Ne. 27:4-5, Morm. 1:13-19.)

5. [2] And the vision of all is become unto you as the words of a book that is sealed. (11) *The coming forth of the Book of Mormon in the last days.* (See 2 Ne. 27:6-8, JS Hist. 2:34.)

6. [2] The words of the book shall be delivered to one that is learned, saying Read this, I pray thee: and he saith I cannot, for it is sealed. (11-12) *The Professor Anthon incident.* (See 2 Ne. 27:9-10, 15-22; JS Hist. 1:64-65.)

7. [3] Wherefore the Lord said, the people draw near me with their mouth, and with their lips do honour me, but have removed their heart far from me. (13) *Christ's words to Joseph Smith in his first vision,* in which he was warned not to join any of the churches then in existence. (See 2 Ne. 27:25, JS Hist. 1:19.)

8. [3] I will do a marvelous work and a wonder among this people. (14) *The restoration of the gospel.* (See 2 Ne. 27:26.)

9. [2] The deaf shall hear the words of the book, and the eyes of the blind shall see out of darkness. (18) *The carrying of the words of the Book of Mormon to the deaf and blind.* (See 2 Ne. 27:29.)

10. [30-31] Lebanon shall be a fruitful field. (15-17)

11. [42] The wicked will be cut off. (19-21)

12. [38] Jacob shall sanctify the name of the Lord and learn doctrine. (22-24)

God Will Pour out His Judgments

Chapter 18—Desolation in the Americas.[3]

1. Woe to the land identified in this manner:

   A. Shadowing with wings. (1) (*The American continents form the image of two wings.*)

   B. Beyond Ethiopia. (1) (*As seen from Palestine.*)

   C. That sends ambassadors by sea in vessels of bulrushes. (2) (*Many pipes?*)

   D. The messengers will go to a nation scattered and peeled. (2) (*American missionaries will be sent to gather Israel.*)

   E. That lifts up an ensign. (3) (*The Church was restored in America.*)

   F. The ensign is lifted up upon the mountains. (3)

2. [14] They shall be cut off and left for the fowls and the beasts to eat. (4-6) (*Destruction in the Americas—the Lord's desolating scourge?*)

3. (22) In that time the nation scattered and peeled shall be brought unto Mount Zion. (7) (See D&C 115:6.)

Chapter 54—The Coming of the Ten Tribes to the New Jerusalem (In America).

Note: A. The chronological determination for the interpretation of this passage is found in 3 Ne. 21:14-22:1. This passage also shows that Is. 54 is to find its fulfillment in the Americas.

   B. This chapter was quoted by the Savior to the Nephites. (See 3 Ne. 22.)

1. [22] The children of the desolate are more than the children of the married wife. (1) (*When the ten tribes come to the New Jerusalem they will outnumber the members of the Church gathered there.*)

2. [22] Thy seed shall inhabit the desolate cities of the Gentiles. (2-3) (*The ten tribes will find vacated cities in the New Jerusalem area of Missouri and will occupy them.*)

3. [22] Though the Lord has hidden His face from Israel for a moment, He will remember and comfort His people in that day. (4-10)

4. [20] The Lord will lay thy stones with fair colours, and thy foundations with sapphires. (11-12) (*The ten tribes will aid in the construction of the beautiful New Jerusalem.*)

---

[3] For further explanation and original sources for the interpretation of this prophecy, see *Prophecy—Key to the Future*, pp. 38-39.

5. [23] Thy children shall be taught of the Lord. Thou shalt not fear. (13-14) (*The Lord will teach the people when He comes to the New Jerusalem temple.*)

6. [25] Enemies will gather against them, but not by the Lord. No weapon that is formed against them shall prosper. (15-17)

Chapter 49—The Second "Servant Song"—The Coming of the Ten Tribes to the New Jerusalem and Their Removal to Palestine.

Note: This chapter is quoted in 1 Nephi 21 and 2 Nephi 6:6-7. 1 Nephi 22 aids in its interpretation.

1. Though Israel be not gathered, yet shall I be glorious in the eyes of the Lord. (5)

2. [22] The Lord will raise up the tribes of Jacob and restore the preserved of Israel. (6)

Note: Another clue—the people of whom the Lord is speaking are still associated together in tribes.

3. [22] The Lord will also be a light to the Gentiles and the salvation for all the earth. (6)

Note: In addition to helping these tribes, the Lord will also be a light unto the Gentiles. When else do we know of a group of tribes being associated with the Gentiles except when they come and mingle with the converted Gentiles in the New Jerusalem? (See 3 Ne. 21:14, 22-26.)

4. The Lord shall be worshiped by kings and princes. (7)

5. [22] The Lord will cause them to inherit the desolate heritages. (8)

Note: When the Ten Tribes come to the New Jerusalem area, they are to inherit the nearby cities which have been left desolate. (See Is. 54:22, 3 Ne. 21:26-22:3.)

6. [22] The Lord will lead his people. He will make all His mountains a way, and His highways shall be exalted. (9-11) (See D&C 133:26-29.)

7. [22] These shall come from far: from the north and from the west, and from the land of Sinim (location unknown). (12-13)

8. [22] Thy destroyers and they that made thee waste shall go forth of thee. (17) (See D&C 133:28.)

9. [22] The waste and desolate places they inherit will be too crowded for them. They will object to them and the people there. (18-21)

Note: Is this the reason why the Ten Tribes move from the New Jerusalem to Palestine?

The Gathering of Israel to Palestine

Chapter 52—The Return and Redemption of Israel.

Note: This passage is quoted in 3 Nephi 20 and Mosiah 15:8-10.

1. [24, 38] Put on thy strength, O Zion. (1) (See Moro. 10:31.)

Note: This passage is interpreted in the Doctrine and Covenants as follows:

> *What is meant by the command in Isaiah, 52nd Chapter, 1st verse, which saith: Put on thy strength, O Zion—and what people had Isaiah reference to?*
>
> *He had reference to those whom God should call in the last days, who should hold the power of priesthood to bring again Zion, and the redemption of Israel; and to put on her strength is to put on the authority of the priesthood, which she, Zion, has a right to by lineage; also to return to that power which she had lost.* (D&C 113:7-8)

2. [30] Loose thyself from the bands of thy neck, O captive daughter of Zion. (2)

Note: This passage is interpreted in the Doctrine and Covenants as follows:

> *What are we to understand by Zion loosing herself from the bands of her neck; 2nd verse?*
>
> *We are to understand that the scattered remnants are exhorted to return to the Lord from whence they have fallen; which if they do, the promise of the Lord is that he will speak to them, or give them revelation. See the 6th, 7th, and 8th verses. The bands of her neck are the curses of God upon her, or the remnants of Israel in their scattered condition among the Gentiles.* (D&C 113:9-10)

3. Since his people have been oppressed, the Lord will redeem them. (3-6)

4. [24] How beautiful upon the mountains are the feet of him that bringeth good tidings by telling Zion that God reigneth! (7) (See Mos. 15:13-18.)

5. [30] The Lord will redeem the waste places of Jerusalem and all the nations shall see His salvation together. (8-10)

6. [30-31] Israel will be called out of wickedness and God will protect her in her return. (11-12)

7. (III) The beginning of the fourth "Servant Song." (13-15)

Note: This passage is considered in Section III.

Chapter 35—The Desert Shall Blossom as the Ransomed of the Lord Returns.

Note: This prophecy is often interpreted as referring to the Saints in the United States. The use of the phrase "the desert shall rejoice, and blossom as the rose" has been especially common among members of the Church as a reference to the productivity of the valleys of Utah. Certainly a parallel can be drawn between the growth and development of the Utah area and the prophesied growth and development of Palestine. Yet Isaiah clearly had reference to the Palestine area when he made the prophecy. Note that the identifying places he mentions are areas in northern Palestine: "The glory of Lebanon shall be given unto it, the excellency of Carmel and Sharon, they shall see the glory of the Lord . . ." (35:2)

1. [30-31] The desert shall rejoice, and blossom as the rose. (1-2)
2. [30-31] The weak will be strengthened in their journey (to Zion). (3-6)
3. [30-31] Waters and streams will break out in the desert. (6-7)
4. [30-31] A highway shall be there, called the way of holiness, and the ransomed of the Lord shall return to Zion. (8-10)

Chapter 27—Israel Shall Be Gathered and Fill the World With Fruit.

1. [30-31] Israel shall blossom and bud, and fill the world with fruit. (1-6)
2. The Lord has not punished Israel with the same severity as He has other nations. (7-11)
3. [30-31] Israel shall be gathered and worship in Jerusalem. (12-13)

David The Prince

Chapter 55—The Rule of David the Prince.

Note: A portion of this chapter is quoted in 2 Nephi 26.

1. An invitation to Christ. (1-2)
2. [32] Prince David will rule. (3-6)
    A. He will be a witness to the people. (4)
    B. He will be a leader and commander. (4)
    C. He shall call a nation he does not know. (4)
    D. Nations which don't know him, shall run unto him. (5)
    E. The Lord will glorify him. (5)
3. Seek the Lord. He will abundantly pardon. (6-7)

4. God's ways and thoughts are not the same as man's. (8-11)

5. [30-31] The land shall be fertile. (12-13)

Chapter 11—The Rod and Branch and the Gathering to Palestine.

Note: This chapter was quoted in its entirety by Moroni to Joseph Smith. Moroni told him that "it was about to be fulfilled." (JS Hist. 1:40) It is also quoted in 2 Ne. 21.

1. [32?] A rod and branch shall come out of the stem of Jesse. (1-5)

    A. He shall have the spirit of the Lord. (2)

    B. He shall judge the poor and meek with righteousness. (3-4)

    C. [35?] He shall slay the wicked. (4)

Note:

A. The rod and branch are probably the same person. This is probably synonymous parallelism.[4]

B. The Doctrine and Covenants gives these items of interpretation:

    (1) The stem is Christ. (D&C 113:1-2)

    (2) The rod is "a servant in the hands of Christ, who is partly a descendant of Jesse as well as of Ephraim, or of the house of Joseph, on whom there is laid much power." (D&C 113:3-4)

C. 2 Ne. 30:1-15 sheds light on the passage. In the context it is shown that these events will precede the time in question: (1) the Book of Mormon will come forth from the Gentiles to the Lamanites (v. 3-4), (2) the Lamanites will accept the gospel (v. 5-6),[5] (3) the Jews will gather in and begin to believe in Christ (v. 7-8),[8] then the passage says:

And with righteousness shall the Lord God judge the poor, and reprove with equity for the meek of the earth. And he shall smite the earth with the rod of his mouth; and with the breath of his lips shall he slay the wicked. For the time speedily cometh that the Lord God shall cause a great division among the people, and the wicked will he destroy; and he will spare his people, yea, even if it so be that he must destroy the wicked by fire. And righteousness shall be the girdle of his loins, and faithfulness the girdle of his reins. (2 Ne. 30:9-11)

---

[4] Synonymous parallelism is a common technic used in Hebrew poetry in which one line expresses a thought and the next line repeats the same thought in different words.

[5] Item 21 on the list of events of the last days.

[6] Item 30 on the list of events of the last days.

Note that in the Book of Mormon passage it is the Lord, not the rod (the servant in the hands of Christ, of D&C 113:3-4) who judges and smites, yet Isaiah clearly states that it is the rod who does this. (This is not a serious dilemma if we realize that the rod will be acting as Christ's agent so they will both judge and smite.)

2. [44] Peace during the millennium. (6-9) (See D&C 29:11.)

3. [44?] In that day there shall be a root of Jesse, which shall stand for an ensign; to it shall the Gentiles seek. (10)

Note:

A.   The Doctrine and Covenants gives this interpretation:

(1) The root is "a descendant of Jesse, as well as of Joseph, unto whom rightly belongs the priesthood, and the keys of the kingdom, for an ensign and for the gathering of my people in the last days." (D&C 113:5-6)

B.   Some interpretive questions with theoretical answers:

(1) Is the **rod** of Is. 11:1 the same person as the **root** of Is. 11:10?

Some say yes, pointing out that they are described as being descendants of both Jesse and Joseph in D&C 113.

Some say no, asserting that the rod is a descendant of the root (Is. 11:1). Thus, their lineage is the same but they are different individuals.

(2) Is the root Joseph Smith?

Some say yes, and assert these bits of evidence in interpretation of Is. 11:10:

A.   Joseph Smith restored the Church which has stood as an ensign. (See D&C 64:37-42.)

B.   He brought in the fulness of the Gentiles and the Gentiles joined themselves to him. (See D&C 45:28.)

C.   He held the priesthood and the keys of the kingdom for the gathering in the last days. (See D&C 27:12-13, 110:11.)

Some say no, if **the root and the rod are the same person,** because:

A.   The rod apparently smites his enemies. This was not characteristic of the Prophet Joseph.

B.   The rod apparently lives into the millennium, which Joseph Smith did not do.

C.   If the root lives on into the millennium, his time will be after the time of the Gentiles is fulfilled. Thus the Gentiles probably would not see him.

(3) Could it be that the rod and the root are separate individuals; that the root is Joseph Smith and the rod is David, the prince who will rule in Palestine during the Battle of Armageddon?

This is the answer that fits best. In this way Joseph Smith meets the qualifications set forth in question 2 above, and David meets the qualifications of the rod who judges in righteousness, yet slays the wicked (in the Battle of Armageddon) and lives into the millennium.

4. [30-31] Israel and Judah shall be gathered to Palestine. (11-12)[7]

5. [34] Israel and Judah will unite and stand together against their enemies. (13-16)

The Battle of Armageddon

Chapter 51—The Battle of Armageddon and the Lord's Eternal Righteousness.

Note: This chapter is quoted in 2 Nephi 8.

1. Remember Abraham and Sarah. (Just as the Lord blessed this childless couple with a child, He will remember and bless Israel.) (1-2)

2. [30-31] The Lord will comfort Zion, and make her waste places fertile. (3)

3. [48, 49] The heavens shall vanish and the earth shall wax old like a garment, but the Lord's salvation will continue forever. (4-6)

4. [42 or 45, 48] The wicked shall be destroyed, but the Lord's righteousness shall be forever. (7-8)

5. A plea for the Lord to aid Israel as He did when He brought them out of Egypt. (9-10)

Note:

"Rahab"— poetical name for Egypt which means "proud."

"dragon"—probably a symbolic representation of Egypt.

6. [30-31] The Lord will help Israel to return with joy and singing. (11-16)

7. [35] Jerusalem will drink the cup of the Lord's fury. (17-18)

---

[7] For a map identifying the nations mentioned here see *Prophecy-Key to the Future*, p. 136.

8. [35] These two things are come unto thee: Thy sons will lie in the streets of Jerusalem, who have been full of fury of the Lord. (1920) (See 2 Ne. 8:19-20, Rev. 11:1-13.)

9. [35] The Lord will take His fury from Israel and place it on those who afflict her. (22-23)

Chapter 4—The Glory of Jerusalem During the Rule of David the Prince Following the Battle of Armageddon.

Note: This chapter is quoted in 2 Nephi 14.

1. (II?) Seven women shall take hold of one man, seeking to be called by his name. (1)

Note: It is doubtful that this verse is referring to a latter-day period, for it seems to fit into the context of Chapter 3, but not into that of Chapter 4. See discussion of the passage under Section II, pp. 59-60.

2. [32] In that day (the day when there will be those of Israel who have escaped) shall the branch of the Lord be beautiful. (2)

Note: The branch is apparently the prince, David, who is to rule in Palestine in the last days. (See Is. 11:1-5, then D&C 113:4)[8]

3. [38] He that is left in Jerusalem (after the Lord has purged its filth by judgment and burning) shall be called holy. (3)

4. [35] The Lord will purge Jerusalem. (3-4)

Note:

A. The previous context of the chapter places this event as following the purge of Jerusalem, apparently in the interval between Christ's coming to the temple in Jerusalem and His coming in glory.

B. Some L.D.S. interpreters have cited this as reference to the city of New Jerusalem in Missouri, based on D&C 84:2. Though their interpretation may be valid, what purge is to take place in that city which will cause the people to escape? How do they understand the "branch" as being in the New Jerusalem instead of in Palestine?

5. [39] The Lord will place his glory (smoke or fire) upon Zion as a defense. (5-6)

---

[8] For a detailed discussion of the identity of the "branch," see *Prophecy—Key to the Future*, pp. 179-182.

The Third and Fourth Periods of Missionary Labor and the Glory of Israel

Chapter 62—The Righteousness of Jerusalem After Israel Is Restored to Palestine.

1. [39] The Lord will not rest until the righteousness of Jerusalem goes forth as brightness, and the salvation thereof as a lamp that burneth. (1)

2. Israel will no longer be called Desolate, but will have a new name: Hephzibah (Hĕph´-zi-băh), meaning "my delight is in her." (1-5)

3. The Lord's servants (angels?) will give Him no rest till He make Jerusalem a praise. (6-7)

4. [41] The good things of Palestine will no longer be given to enemies. (8-9)

5. [30-31] Cast up the highway, lift up a standard for the people. (10)

6. [30-31] The Lord will send a message throughout the world to Israel that His salvation cometh. (11)

7. [41] They shall call them The Holy People, the redeemed of the Lord. (12)

Chapter 60—The Glory of Israel in Palestine Following Christ's Coming to the Jerusalem Temple.

1. [39] The glory of the Lord is upon Israel, yet gross darkness covers the people of the earth. (1-2)

2. [41] The Gentiles and kings shall come to thy light. (3-4)

3. [41] The abundance of the sea shall be given to Israel; the surrounding nations will bring their treasures. (5-8)

4. Thy sons shall come from far with treasure because the Lord hath glorified thee. (9)

5. [41] The sons of strangers shall build up thy walls, and their kings shall minister unto thee. (10-11)

6. [41] The nation and kingdom that will not serve thee shall perish. (12)

7. [33] Wood from Lebanon will be brought to adorn the sanctuary. (13-17)

8. [41] Those that despised Israel and the sons of those that afflicted her will bow down to her. (14)

9. [41] Thou shalt suck the milk of the Gentiles and kings. (16)

10. [41] Violence shall no more be heard in the land. (18)

11. [39] The glory of the Lord shall be there and provide light. (19-20)

12. [41] A little one shall become a thousand, and a small one a strong nation. (21-22)

Chapter 61—The Seed of Israel to Be Ministers Among the Gentiles.

1. (III) The Lord will proclaim the acceptable year of the Lord. (1:2) (See Lk. 4:16-21.)

Note: This passage is considered in Section III.

2. [30-31] They shall build the old waste and desolate cities, while strangers tend their flocks. (3-5)

3. [40, 41] Men will call the people of Israel the ministers of God; their seed will be known among the Gentiles. (6-9)

4. [40, 41] The Lord will cause righteousness and praise to spring forth before all the nations. (10-11)

Chapter 66—Missionary Work Following the Battle of Armageddon.

1. The heaven is the Lord's throne, the earth His footstool; Where is His house for him here on the earth? (1-2)

2. (I) The outward sacrifices of Israel are an abomination before God. (3-4)

3. [37] The Lord shall appear to your joy. There will be noise from the city and the temple as the Lord renders recompense to his enemies. (5-6)

4. [30-31] Israel travailed and brought forth a man child before her pain came. (7-8)

Note: Some interpret the man-child as being the newly established nation of Israel. The nation of Israel is established before the pain of her cleansing in the battle of Armageddon.

5. [41] Jerusalem shall be comforted. She shall have peace like a river and the glory of the Gentiles like a flowing stream. (9-13)

6. [35] The Lord will show His indignation upon His enemies, and the slain of the Lord shall be many. (14-17)

7. [41] The nations will gather to Jerusalem to see the Lord's glory. Those that have escaped will be sent to the nations to declare the glory of God among the Gentiles. (18-19)

8. [41] The nations will help bring the remaining members of Israel as an offering to the Lord. (19-21)

9. [44] The Lord will create a new heaven and a new earth. (22)

10. [41] Israel's seed and all flesh will come up to worship him. (22-23)

11. [35] Men will see the carcasses of those who have transgressed against the Lord. (24)

Chapter 12—Praise to Jehovah.

Note: This chapter is quoted in 2 Nephi 22.

1. [41] A song of praise unto God when his goodness is known throughout all the earth. (1-6)

Christ's Coming in Glory

Chapter 40—The Incomparable Glory of the Lord Will Be Revealed.

1. [42] Every valley shall be exalted, and every mountain and hill shall be made low. (3-4)

2. [42] The glory of the Lord shall be revealed, and all flesh shall see it together. (5)

3. [42] Temporal things will wither but the word of God shall stand forever. (6-8)

4. [44] The Lord God will rule from Jerusalem. (9-11)

5. The Lord has controlled the earth and has knowledge. (12-14)

6. There is no one that can be likened unto God. Men are insignificant beside Him. (15-25)

7. The Lord is all powerful. He does not faint nor is He weary. (26-28)

8. The Lord gives strength to those that serve Him; they shall run and not be weary, and they shall walk and not faint. (29-31) (cf. D&C 89:20.)

Chapter 2—The Temple in Jerusalem, Christ's Coming in Glory.

Note: This chapter is quoted in 2 Nephi 12.

1. [33, 41] The Lord's house shall be established in the tops of the mountains, and all nations shall flow unto it. (1-3)

Note: This prophecy, together with Mic. 4:1-2, is often quoted by Latter-day Saints as pertaining to the Salt Lake Temple, which is also high in the mountains and has been visited by the people of many nations. While an interesting parallel can be drawn between the prophecy and the Salt Lake Temple, there is no scriptural evidence that Isaiah was speaking of it rather than the temple in Jerusalem. The reader should note that—

A. The preceding verse clearly defines this prophecy as the word of Isaiah concerning Judah and its capital, Jerusalem. (1)

B. The following verse, which is clearly a portion of the prophecy, gives a chronological clue as to when the prophecy will be fulfilled. This is to take place at a time when the Lord will (1) judge among the nations, (2) rebuke many people, and the people will (3) beat their swords into plowshares and (4) cease from waging war. (4) It would seem that this is clearly a prophecy of events immediately preceding the millennial era and of the millennium (See Is. 11:6-9, 65:25), rather than of the past century.

C. "Mountain(s) of the Lord's house" is a phrase which seemingly refers to the dwelling place of God. D&C 133:13 clearly uses the phrase in referring to Jerusalem: "And let them who be of Judah flee unto Jerusalem, unto the mountains of the Lord's house."

D. Isn't the Salt Lake Temple an arbitrary selection as the fulfillment of the prophecy? Why not the temples in Manti, Logan, St. George or others in the mountain West, which all have been visited by people of many nations and which are relatively high above sea level?

2. [44] Out of Zion shall go forth the law, and the word of the Lord from Jerusalem. (3)

Note: This may be a prophecy which refers to the two centers of power in the last days, the New Jerusalem (as Zion) and the old Jerusalem. However, Isaiah consistently used the term Zion as referring to the Palestine Jerusalem. (See Is. 1:26-27, 33:20, 40:9, 41:27, 52:1, etc.) The passage is probably synonymous parallelism, a common Hebrew poetry form in which one line asserts an idea and the next line repeats the same thought in different words. (For other examples, see Ps. 15:1, 10:1, 2:1, and hundreds more.)

3. [44] Nation shall not lift up the sword against nation. (4)

4. (I) The sins of Israel are listed. (5-9)

5. [42] Fear and a terrible earthquake will come when Christ is exalted (His coming in glory). (10-21) (See Morm. 9:2-5.)

Chapter 63—The Lord's Coming in Glory.

1. [42] The Lord will come in His glory, dressed in red apparel, and tread down the wicked. (1-6) (See D&C 133:46-52.)

2. (I) The Lord with loving kindness blessed Israel, but they rebelled against Him. (7-10)

3. (I) Israel then remembered the way the Lord had helped them in days gone by. (10-14)

4. [22] A prayer: Return the tribes to their inheritance. (15-19)

Chapter 64—A Prayer Seeking the Lord's Coming.

1. [42] A prayer that the Lord will cleanse the earth with fire. (1-3)

2. (I) Israel's confession that the Lord does not hear her people because of their wickedness. (4-8)

3. (I) Wilt thou hold thy peace, O Lord, when Jerusalem is a desolation? (9-12)

Chapter 26—The Lord Will Punish the Inhabitants of the Earth For Their Iniquity.

1. [41] We have a strong city where only the righteous may enter. (1-4)

2. [42] The Lord will destroy the wicked because they will not learn righteousness. (5-11)

3. [40-41?] The Lord has made the nation increase. (12-18)

4. [41] Thou art glorified: thou hadst removed the nation far unto all the ends of the earth. We have not wrought any deliverance in the earth, neither have the inhabitants of the world fallen. (15-18)

5. (III) Thy dead men shall live, the earth shall cast out the dead. (19)

6. [42] The Lord will come to punish the inhabitants of the earth for their iniquity. (20-21)

Chapter 24—The Cleansing of the Earth at Christ's Coming.

1. [42] The earth is desolate, with few men left. (1-12)

2. [42] The earth is defiled because the people have transgressed the laws, changed the ordinances, and broken the everlasting covenant. (5-6)

Note: This passage is often included in scripture lists pertaining to the apostasy which took place following New Testament times. While the people did break the laws and changed the ordinances and covenants at that time, there is no indication that Isaiah was prophesying concerning that period here. In chapter 24 the prophet is clearly speaking of another period of apostasy and wickedness which will be evident in the day the Lord cleanses the earth and leaves but few inhabitants—an event which is yet future. This passage should properly be used for purposes of comparison, not as a prophecy of the apostasy which followed New Testament times.

3. [42] The fires of that day will cause the righteous to sing praises to the Lord. (13-15)

4. [42] The earth, in this day shall—
   A. Be utterly broken down. (19)
   B. Be clean dissolved. (19)
   C. Be moved exceedingly. (19)
   D. Reel to and fro like a drunkard. (20)
   E. Be removed like a cottage. (20)
   F. Fall and not rise again. (20)
5. [42] The wicked shall be cast into the (spirit) prison, and shall not be visited for many days. (21-22)
6. [44] The Lord shall reign in mount Zion, and in Jerusalem. (23)

Chapter 34—The Burning of the Earth at Christ's Coming.
1. [42] The Lord has destroyed the armies of all nations. Their dead stink. (1-3)
2. [42] The host of heaven shall be dissolved, and the heavens shall be rolled together as a scroll. (4)
3. [42] The lands shall be turned into unquenchable burning, for it is the day of the Lord's vengeance. (5-10)

Note: These verses may refer to special punishments which will come upon the land of Edom (or Idumea) at the time of the Lord's coming, or they have reference to the entire world, with the term "Idumea" being used to refer to general wickedness. (See D&C 1:36.)

4. [42] The nobles will be removed and thorns will come up in the palaces. (11-15)
5. Read out of the book of the Lord: no one of these (prophecies) shall fail. (16-17)

Chapter 33—The Exaltation of the Lord and the People of Zion.
1. [42] The treacherous spoiler will be spoiled. (1)
2. [42] A prayer:
   A. [35] At the lifting up of the Lord the nations were scattered. His spoil shall be gathered. (2-4)
   B. [41] The Lord is exalted and has filled Zion with judgment and righteousness. (5-6)
   C. [35] The highways lay waste, the earth mourneth and languisheth. (7-9)
3. [42] The Lord is exalted, the wicked are burned with fire. (10-13)

4. [49] The righteous shall dwell (with God) in everlasting burnings. (14-17)

5. [49] Jerusalem shall be a quiet habitation with a tabernacle. It shall not be removed. (18-24)

The Millennium

Chapter 65—The Millennium.

1. Israel does not hear the Lord because of her wickedness. (1-7)

2. [30-31] A seed will inherit the mountains. (8-10)

3. [35] The Lord will punish the wicked among the people of Israel. (11-16)

4. [44] The Lord will create a new heaven and a new earth. (17) (See Rev. 21:1-5.)

5. [44] A child shall live to 100. (18-20)

6. [44] They shall build and enjoy the work of their hands. (21-24)

7. [44] They shall not hurt or destroy; there shall be peace. (25)

Chapter 32—The Peaceful Life of the Millennium.

1. [44] A king shall reign in righteousness, and princes shall rule in judgment. (1-4)

2. [44] No longer will the vile person be honored as good, nor be allowed to destroy the poor with lying words. (5-8)

3. (I) The careless women will be troubled because of their barrenness, the palaces shall be forsaken. (9-14)

4. [44] The spirit shall be poured out from on high and the righteous will dwell in quietness and assurance for ever. (15-20)

Chapter 25—A Hymn of the Lord's Greatness During the Millennium.

1. [35] The Lord has destroyed cities but has aided the poor and the needy. (1-5)

2. [44] He will give the people a feast of fat things (rich blessings). (6)

3. [42] He will rend the veil and reveal himself to the people. (7) (See D&C 67:10, 38:8.)

4. [43] He will swallow up death in victory. (8)

5. [34 ?] The pride of Moab will be brought down. (9-12)

Summary of Isaiah—Section IV

After studying section IV of Isaiah the student should know:

1. Isaiah prophesied of many events in the last days, including:
   - A. The coming forth of the Book of Mormon.
   - B. Destruction in the Americas
   - C. The coming of the Ten Tribes to the New Jerusalem in America.
   - D. The removal of the Ten Tribes to Palestine.
   - E. The gathering of Judah to Palestine.
   - F. Israel's political affairs in the last days.
   - G. David the Prince.
   - H. The building of the Jerusalem Temple.
   - I. The Battle of Armageddon.
   - J. The Third and Fourth periods of missionary labor.
   - K. The glory of Israel.
   - L. Christ's coming in glory.
   - M. The cleansing of the Earth at Christ's coming.
   - N. The Millennium.

2. Isaiah's prophecies are important because they provide a basis for comparison and interpretation with other scriptural prophecies. They are a pattern of scripture with numerous references to most of the major prophetic themes concerning the restoration of Israel.

3. Many of Isaiah's prophecies of the last days are amplified and interpreted in other standard works of the Church.

4. The prophecies of Isaiah are sometimes difficult to assign to their period of prophetic fulfillment because he suddenly skips from one time to another without warning. A key to understanding these skips is to realize that he continually compares one period with another.

5. Care should be taken in interpreting scriptures. The student should be careful to

   A. Find a pattern of scriptures which support and explain each other.

   B. Determine the chronological relationship of the passage to aid in determining the interpretation.

   C. Glean the interpretive clues from the context.

   D. Propose alternative interpretations. Attempt to determine which interpretation the speaker intended when he made the prophecy.

   E. Check interpretations with other scriptures and with Church interpretations.

F. Be aware of the tendency to "force" interpretations so that prophecies of future events are said to apply to present situations.

6. Prophecy of the last days is the most important theme of the book of Isaiah. Twenty-seven of the sixty-six chapters of the book have this as their major subject.

7. The fourth period of prophetic fulfillment is the last days.

And in that day thou shalt say, O LORD, I will praise thee: though thou wast angry with me, thine anger is turned away, and thou comfortedst me.

Behold, God is my salvation; I will trust, and not be afraid: for the LORD JEHOVAH is my strength and my song; he also is become my salvation.

Therefore with joy shall ye draw water out of the wells of salvation.

And in that day shall ye say, Praise the LORD, call upon his name, declare his doings among the people, make mention that his name is exalted.

Sing unto the LORD; for he hath done excellent things: this is known in all the earth.

Cry out and shout, thou inhabitant of Zion: for great is the Holy One of Israel in the midst of thee.

(Isaiah 12:1-6)

Part III

DOCTRINAL ANALYSES

The voice of him that crieth in the wilderness, Prepare ye the way of the LORD, make straight in the desert a highway for our God.

Every valley shall be exalted, and every mountain and hill shall be made low: and the crooked shall be made straight, and the rough places plain:

And the glory of the LORD shall be revealed, and all flesh shall see it together: for the mouth of the LORD hath spoken it.

(Isaiah 40:3-5)

> For the mountains shall depart, and the hills be removed; but my kindness shall not depart from thee, neither shall the covenant of my peace be removed, saith the LORD that hath mercy on thee.
>
> O thou afflicted, tossed with tempest, and not comforted, behold, I will lay thy stones with fair colours, and lay thy foundations with sapphires.
>
> And I will make thy windows of agates, and thy gates of carbuncles, and all thy borders of pleasant stones.
>
> And all thy children shall be taught of the LORD; and great shall be the peace of thy children.
>
> (Isaiah 54:10-13)

8

SIX MAJOR DOCTRINES OF THE OLD TESTAMENT

Scriptures Are Studied So Man Can Apply Basic Teachings

The most important reason for studying the scriptures is to determine the basic teachings which man can use and apply to enrich his life. There is little justification for scriptural study unless applications can be found to improve man's spiritual lot today. The history revealed in scriptural study is also interesting and important, but a knowledge of it is useless unless it can be applied in some manner. As Nephi said concerning the writings of Isaiah, "I did liken all scriptures unto us, that it might be for our profit and learning." (1 Nephi 19:23) The application of eternal principles found in the scriptures to man's present life is a rewarding process. Indeed, the abundance of "spiritual food" in the scriptures is what makes them of such great value to man. It is also the reason why they are so enjoyable to read.

Old Testament's Central Doctrines

Certain doctrines tend to be revealed in greater abundance in some portions of the scriptures than do others. Yet the most important doctrinal themes will be found in all the Standard Works of the Church. Six doctrines comprise the predominant themes of the Old Testament prophets. They are vital to every man who seeks to understand the workings of God and who

desires to comprehend his own relationship with Deity. These doctrines
are:

1. The nature of God and Godhood.
2. The manner in which God communicates with man.
3. The nature of sin.
4. The nature of man's agency and God's judgment.
5. God's program to aid man in living righteously.
6. God's program to prepare the world for His coming in the last
days.

In the six chapters which follow, the above doctrines will be presented with a listing of key statements found in the book of Isaiah pertaining to each of them. Each of the six doctrinal themes will be presented with
an outline of its major sub-divisions.

This list does not represent a complete coverage of the pertinent
passages found in the writings of the Old Testament prophets, but many
important passages are included. Those judged to be major passages are
marked with an asterisk (*).

I will mention the lovingkindnesses of the LORD, and the praises
of the LORD, according to all that the LORD hath bestowed on us, and
the great goodness toward the house of Israel, which he hath
bestowed on them according to his mercies, and according to the
multitude of his lovingkindnesses.

For he said, Surely they are my people, children that will not lie:
so he was their Saviour.

In all their affliction he was afflicted, and the angel of his presence saved them: in his love and in his pity he redeemed them; and
he bare them, and carried them all the days of old.

(Isaiah 63:7-9)

9

THE NATURE OF GOD AND GODHOOD

This doctrine is concerned with the many qualities, attributes, and emotions of God. It is believed that man must understand God to effectively love Him, serve Him, and seek Him in prayer. It becomes obvious that God desires man to know Him and understand His nature and personality, for one can scarcely read a chapter of scripture without finding information which He has revealed about Himself.

In the passages that follow, no effort has been made to differentiate between the Father and the Son. It should be observed, however, that almost all of the verses are references to God the Son, Jehovah. The list is based on an analysis of the prophetic section of the entire Old Testament, with representative references provided. Key passages from the book of Isaiah are listed under the subject headings. Passages regarded as particularly significant are marked with an asterisk (*). Obviously, this is not a comprehensive listing of all relevant passages.

1. God is Accessible and Should be Sought:
(2 Chron. 14:4; 14:7; 15:2*; 26:5; Amos 5:4-5, 8; Hos. 5:15; Is. 8:19; 55:6; Jer. 23:23; 29:12-13*)

1. Should not a people seek unto their God? (8:19)

2. God is All-powerful (Omnipotent):
(Is. 40:13, 14, 15-17, 22, 25-26*, 28; 42:13; Jer. 32:27)

1. Who hath directed the Spirit of the Lord, instructed him, and taught him judgment, knowledge, and understanding? All nations before him are as nothing. (40:13-17)

2. He sitteth upon the circle of the earth, and the inhabitants are as grasshoppers. To whom then will ye liken me, or shall I be equal? (40:22-26)

3. God Allows Man a Choice:
(2 Chron. 13:12; 15:2*; 24:20; Is. 1:19-20*)
   1. If ye be willing and obedient, ye shall eat the good of the land: but if ye refuse and rebel, ye shall be devoured with the sword. (1:19-20)

4. God May Feel Anger, Indignation, Fury, and Wrath:
(1 Ki. 11:9; 15:30; 16:2, 7, 13, 26; 22:53; 2 Ki. 22:17; 23:19, 26; 24:20; 23:26*; 2 Chron. 28:11, 25; Mic. 7:8-9; Is. 12:1; 27:4; 42:25*; 51:20; 60:10; 66:14; Nahum 1:2, 6; Hab. 3:2, 8, 12; Jer. 3:12; 4:4, 26; 6:11; 7:18-20; 8:19; 12:13; 18:23; 21:5; 23:20; 25:7, 15-16, 37-38; 44:6; Lam. 1:12; 2:6; 4:11; 5:22; Ezek. 5:15; 7:3; Zech. 10:3.)
   1. Though thou wast angry with me, thine anger is turned away. (12:1)
   2. Fury is not in me: who would set the briers and thorns against me in battle? (27:4)
   3. Therefore he hath poured upon him the fury of his anger, and it hath set him on fire round about. (42:25)
   4. They are full of the fury of the Lord, the rebuke of thy God. (51:20)
   5. For in my wrath I smote thee, but in my favour have I mercy on thee. (60:10)
   6. The hand of the Lord shall be known toward his servants, and his indignation toward his enemies. (66:14)

5. God May Appear unto Man:
(1 Ki. 11:9; 22:19-23; 2 Chron. 18:18-22; Amos 9:1; Is. 6:1-13; Ezek. 1:1, 26-28; 3:23-24; Dan. 3:25)
   1. I saw the Lord sitting upon a throne, high and lifted up; mine eyes have seen the King, the Lord of hosts. (6:1-5)

6. God May be Astonished: (Jer. 8:21)

7. God May Avenge or Take Vengeance:
(Jer. 5:9, 29; 9:9; 50:15; Nahum 1:2)

8. God has Beauty: (Zech. 9:17)

9. God May Give Comfort and Compassion:
(2 Ki. 13:23; Is. 12:1; 49:13; Jer. 12:15; 31:3; Lam. 3:22, 23)

1. Though thou wast angry with me, thine anger is turned away, and thou comfortest me. (12:1)

10. God Controls the Actions and Fate of Individuals:
(1 Ki. 11:14, 21, 34*, 36; 12:15; 20:42; 22:20-23; 2 Ki. 3:10*; 9:7; 10:30; 15:5, 12; 19:7; 24:20; 2 Chron. 10:15; 11:4; 13:20; 15:6-7; 16:7, 8; 18:31; 21:18; 25:16, 20; 26:16-20; 28:19; 33:11; 36:22; Mic. 7:8-9; Is. 29:10; 63:17; Ezek. 24:16-18; Ezra 7:6; Dan. 1:9, 17; 2:37; 4:17, 25, 32; Zech. 8:10)

1. The Lord hath poured out upon you the spirit of deep sleep, and hath closed your eyes: the prophets and your rulers, the seers hath he covered. (29:10)

2. O Lord, why hast thou made us to err from thy ways, and hardened our heart from thy fear? (63:17)

11. God Controls the Actions and Fate of Nations:
(1 Ki. 12:24; 14:14; 20:13, 23; 2 Ki. 3:18; 8:19; 10:32; 13:5; 15:37*; 17:20*; 19:34; 21:14; 24:2*, 3*; 2 Chron. 13:15-16*; 20:6-7, 27; 24:24*; 29:8; 30:12; 32:21; 36:17; Mic. 1:6; Is. 3:1-3; 7:20; Obad. 2, 4, 8; Jer. 5:15-17; 6:8; 7:3-7; 12:12, 17; 14:12; 15:4; 19:7; 20:5; 21:4-6, 7*; 22:7; 25:9, 12; 27:8; 32:3; 46:26; Ezek. 20:18-26; 29:19; 30:23-24; 38:16; 39:1-2; Dan. 1:1-2; 2:21)

1. The Lord doth take away from Jerusalem and Judah the whole stay of bread and water, the mighty man, the judge, the prophet, the prudent, the honorable man. (3:1-3)

2. The Lord shall shave (Israel and Syria) with a razor that is hired, the king of Assyria. (7:20)

12. God Controls Nature and the Elements:
(2 Ki. 8:1; Jon. 1:4, 17; 4:6, 8; Amos 4:7-10*, 13; 5:8; 8:9; 9:5, 6; Is. 23:11; 29:6*; 42:15; 43:16; 44:3; 50:2; 51:10, 15; Nahum 1:3, 4; Hab. 3:6-11; Jer. 3:3; 5:22, 24; 10:10, 13*; 14:22; Dan. 2:22; Neh. 9:11; Joel 2:23)

1. He stretched out his hand over the sea. (23:11)

2. Thou shalt be visited of the Lord of hosts with thunder, earthquake, storm and tempest, and devouring fire. (29:6)

13. God Covenants With His People:
(2 Ki. 11:17; 2 Chron. 21:7*; Is. 54:10; 61:8; Dan. 9:4; Neh. 1:5; 9:32)

1. My kindness shall not depart from thee, neither shall the covenant of my peace be removed, saith the Lord. (54:10)

14. God is a Creator:
(Jon. 1:9; Amos 4:13; 5:8; Is. 37:16*; 40:12; 41:19-20; 42:5*; 43:15; 44:2, 24*; 45:7, 12; 48:13; 51:13; 64:8; Jer. 10:12; 27:5; 32:17; Neh. 9:6; Zech. 12:1)

1. O Lord of hosts, thou hast made heaven and earth. (37:16)

2. Who hath measured the waters, and meted out heaven, and weighed the mountains and the hills? (40:12)

3. I will plant the cedar, myrtle, the fir tree, and the pine, that they may see that the hand of the Lord hath done this and hath created it. (41:19-20)

4. Thus saith God the Lord, he that created the heavens, and spread forth the earth, and giveth breath to the people upon it. (42:5)

5. I am the Lord, your Holy One, the creator of Israel, your King. (43:15)

6. Thus saith the Lord that made thee, that formed thee from the womb. (44:2)

7. Thus saith the Lord, thy redeemer, and he that formed thee from the womb, I am the Lord that maketh all things; the heavens and earth. (44:24)

8. I form the light, and create darkness: I make peace, and create evil: I the Lord do all these things. I have made the earth, and created man upon it. (45:7, 12)

9. Mine hand hath laid the foundation of the earth, and my right hand spanned the heavens. (48:13)

10. Forgettest thou the Lord thy maker, that hath stretched forth the heavens, and laid the foundations of the earth? (51:13)

11. O Lord, thou art our father; we are the clay, and thou our potter; and we all are the work of thy hand. (64:8)

15. God is Eternal:
(Is. 40:8; 51:6, 8; Lam. 5:19; Dan. 4:3, 34; 6:26-27)

1. The grass withereth, the flower fadeth: but the word of our God shall stand forever. (40:8)

2. The heavens shall vanish away, and the earth shall wax old, and they that dwell therein shall die, but my salvation shall be forever, and my righteousness shall not be abolished. My righteousness shall be forever. (51:6, 8)

16. God is Faithful:
(Is. 49:7)

1. Kings shall see and arise, princes also shall worship, because of the Lord that is faithful. (49:7)

17. God is the Father of Man:
(Is. 63:16; Jer. 3:19; Mal. 1:6; 2:10)

1. Doubtless thou art our father. Thou, O Lord, art our father, our redeemer; thy name is from everlasting. (63:16)

18. God Never Forgets Men's Works: (Amos 8:7)

19. God Forgives and Pardons:
(2 Chron. 12:7, 12; 32:26; Mic. 7:18-20*; Is. 1:18*; 38:17; 43:25; 44:22; 55:7; Jer. 31:34; 33:8; Lam. 3:42; Dan. 9:9; Neh. 9:17)

1. Though your sins be as scarlet, they shall be as white as snow. (1:18)

2. Thou hast in love to my soul delivered it from the pit of corruption: for thou hast cast all my sin behind thy back. (38:17)

3. I am he that blotteth out thy transgressions for mine own sake, and will not remember thy sins. (43:25)

4. I have blotted out thy transgressions and thy sins: return unto me; for I have redeemed thee. (44:22)

5. Let the wicked return unto the Lord, and he will have mercy upon him; for he will abundantly pardon. (55:7)

20. God Gives His Servants Power to Perform Miracles:
(1 Ki. 13:4-6; 18:36-38; 2 Ki. 1:9-12; 2:8, 14; 2:11; 4:18-37; 13:21)

21. God has Glory:
(Is. 6:3; 42:8; 66:1; Hag. 1:8)

1. Holy is the Lord of hosts: the whole earth is full of his glory. (6:3)

2. I am the Lord: and my glory will I not give to another, neither my praise to graven images. (42:8)

3. Thus saith the Lord, the heaven is my throne, and the earth is my footstool. (66:1)

22. God is Good: (Ezra 3:11; Zech. 9:17)

23. God is Gracious:
(2 Ki. 13:23; 2 Chron. 30:9; Jon. 4:2; Neh. 9:17, 31; Joel 2:13)

24. God May Feel Grief: (Jer. 10:19)

25. God Guides Man:
(Is. 11:2-3*; 48:17; 49:10; 50:4; 55:3, 10-11; 61:8*; Jer. 14:9; Ezek. 2:2; Neh. 9:20)

1. The spirit of the Lord shall rest upon him, wisdom, understanding, counsel and might, knowledge and the fear of the Lord, and shall make him of quick understanding in the fear of the Lord. (11:2-3)

2. I am the Lord thy God which teacheth thee to profit, which leadeth thee by the way that thou shouldest go. (48:17)

3. He that hath mercy on them shall lead them, even by the springs of water shall he guide them. (49:10)

4. The Lord God hath given me the tongue of the learned, that I should know how to speak a word in season; he wakeneth mine ear to hear as the learned. (50:4)

5. Incline your ear, and hear; my word shall accomplish that which I please, and it shall prosper in the thing whereto I sent it. (55:3, 10-11)

6. I will direct their work in truth, and I will make an everlasting covenant with them. (61:8)

26. God May Hate: (Mal. 1:2-3)

27. God Hears and Answers Prayers:
(2 Ki. 20:5; 2 Chron. 33:11-13; Jon. 2:2, 7; Mic. 7:7; Is. 38:2-3, 5-8; 41:14; Lam. 3:57)

1. Hezekiah pleads with the Lord to hear his prayer. The Lord sends Isaiah to tell him, I have heard thy prayer, I have seen thy tears, behold, I will add unto thy days fifteen years. (38:2-3, 5-8)

2. Fear not, ye men of Israel; I will help thee, saith the Lord, and thy redeemer. (41:14)

28. God is Helpful:
(2 Chron. 14:11; 32:7-8; Is. 41:10, 13*, 14)

1. Fear thou not, for I am with thee: be not dismayed: I will strengthen thee; yea, I will help thee; yea, I will uphold thee with the right hand of my righteousness. (41:10, 13-14)

29. God is Holy:
(Is. 5:16, 6:3; 43:3)

1. God that is holy shall be sanctified in righteousness. (5:16)
2. Holy, holy, holy is the Lord of hosts. (6:3)
3. I am the Lord thy God, the Holy One of Israel, thy Saviour. (43:3)

30. God May be Hurt: (Jer. 8:21; 10:19)

31. God May be Jealous: (1 Ki. 14:22; Nahum 1:2; Joel 2:18)

32. God Will Judge and Bring Judgment:
(Mic. 4:3-4; Is. 16:5; 61:8; Jer. 1:16; 9:24; Lam. 3:59)

1. In mercy shall the throne be established: and he shall sit upon it in truth, judging, and seeking judgment, and hasting righteousness. (16:5)

2. I the Lord love judgment, I hate robbery, I will direct their work in truth. (61:8)

33. God is Kind:
(Jon. 4:2; Is. 43:20; 54:8, 10; 63:7; Jer. 9:24; Neh. 9:17; Joel 2:13)

1. I give waters in the wilderness, and rivers in the desert, to give drink to my people, my chosen. (43:20)

2. In a little wrath I hid my face from thee for a moment; but with everlasting kindness will I have mercy on thee, saith the Lord thy Redeemer. My kindness shall not depart from thee, neither shall the covenant of my peace be removed. (54:8, 10)

3. I will mention the lovingkindnesses of the Lord, according to all that the Lord hath bestowed upon us, and the great goodness toward the house of Israel which he hath bestowed upon them. (63:7)

34. God Knows Man's Thoughts and Acts:
(2 Ki. 19:27; 2 Chron. 16:9*; Jon. 1:2; 3:10; Amos 4:13; 5:12*; 9:8; Mic. 1:2; Is. 37:28*; 66:18; Nahum 1:7; Jer. 2:2, 34; 5:3; 12:3; 16:17*; 17:10; 21:10; 23:24; 29:23; 32:19*; Zech. 4:10)

1. I know thy abode, and thy going out, and thy coming in, and thy rage against me. (37:28)

2. I know their works and their thoughts. (66:18)

35. God Loves:
(Is. 38:17; Jer. 9:24; 31:13; 32:18; Mal. 1:2-3)

1. I had great bitterness: but thou hast in love to my soul delivered it from the pit of corruption: for thou hast cast all my sins behind thy back. (38:17)

36. God is Merciful:
(2 Chron. 20:21; 30:9*; Jon. 4:2; Mic. 7:18-20*; Is. 14:1; 16:5; 49:10, 13; 54:7, 8, 10; 55:7; 60:10; Hab. 3:2; Jer. 3:12; 31:20; 33:11; 42:12; Lam. 3:22, 23; Ezra 3:11; 9:9; Dan. 9:9; Neh. 1:5; 9:17, 31; Zech. 1:16; Joel 2:13)

1. For the Lord will have mercy on Jacob, and will yet choose Israel, and set them in their own land. (14:1)

2. And in mercy shall the throne be established. (16:5)

3. For he that hath mercy shall lead them, even by the springs of water shall he guide them. For the Lord hath comforted his people, and will have mercy upon his afflicted. (49:10, 13)

4. With great mercies shall I gather you, with everlasting kindness will I have mercy on thee, saith the Lord that hath mercy upon thee. (54:7-8, 10)

5. Let the wicked return unto the Lord, and he will have mercy upon him. (55:7)

6. In my wrath I smote thee, but in my favour have I had mercy upon thee. (60:10)

37. God is No Respecter of Persons: (2 Chron. 19:7)

38. God is the Only God With Whom Man Is to be Concerned:
(Hos. 13:4; Is. 37:16; 41:4; 42:8; 43:10-11, 13; 44:6, 8; 45:18, 22; 46:9; 48:11-12)

1. Thou art the God, even thou alone. (37:16)

2. Who hath wrought and done it, calling the generations from the beginning? I the Lord, the first, and with the last, I am he. (41:4)

3. I am the Lord: and my glory will I not give to another. (42:8)

4. Ye are my witnesses; before me there was no God formed, neither shall there be after me; beside me there is no Savior. Before the day was I am he. (43:10-11, 13)

5. Thus saith the Lord the King of Israel, and the redeemer the Lord of hosts; I am the first, and I am the last; and beside me there is no God. Is there a God beside me? yea, there is no God; I know not any. (44:6, 8)

6. Thus saith the Lord that formed the earth and made it; I am the Lord; and there is none else. I am God, and there is none else. (45:18, 22)

7. I am God, and there is none else; I am God, and there is none like me. (46:9)

8. I will not give my glory unto another. I am he; I am the first, I also am the last. (48:11-12)

39. God May Feel Pain: (Jer. 4:19)

40. God May Praise: (Jer. 33:9)

41. God has Purpose:
(Is. 43:7; 45:18, 23)

1. I have created him for my glory, I have formed him, yea, I have made him. (43:7)

2. Thus saith God that formed the earth; he created it not in vain, he formed it to be inhabited. Unto me every knee shall bow, every tongue shall swear. (45:18, 23)

42. God Is a Redeemer of Man:

(Is. 43:1, 3; 44:22; 47:4; 49:26; 53:5-6, 8, 9, 10, 11, 12; 63:9, 16; Jer. 14:8; Lam. 3:58)

1. I have redeemed thee; thou art mine. I am the Lord thy God, thy Saviour. (43:1,3)

2. Return unto me, for I have redeemed thee. (44:22)

3. As for our redeemer, the Lord of hosts is his name, the Holy One of Israel. (47:4)

4. All flesh shall know that I the Lord am thy Saviour and thy Redeemer, the mighty one of Jacob. (49:26)

5. He was wounded for our transgressions, the Lord hath laid upon him the iniquity of us all. (53:5-6)

6. By his knowledge shall my righteous servant justify many; for he shall bear their iniquities. (53:11)

7. He was numbered with the transgressors; and he bare the sins of many, and made intercession for the transgressors. (53:12)

43. God Provides Refuge:

(Is. 8:13-14; 25:4; Nahum 1:7)

1. Sanctify the Lord of hosts, and he shall be for a sanctuary. (8:13-14)

2. Thou hast been a strength to the poor, a strength to the needy in his distress, a refuge from the storm, when the blast of the terrible ones is as a storm against the wall. (25:4)

44. God is a Revelator:

(1 Ki. 19:12; 22:14; 2 Ki. 17:13; 21:10; Jon. 1:2; 3:2; Amos 3:6-8; 7:14-15; Hos. 12:10; Is. 6:8; 43:12; 44:26; 45:11; 46:9-11; 48:3, 4-5, 16; Jer. 33:6; Ezek. 1:3; 2:6-7; 3:11; 3:18-22; 12:21-25; Dan. 2:18-19, 20-22, 28, 29, 45; Neh. 9:13-14)

1. I heard the voice of the Lord, saying, Whom shall I send, and who will go for us? (6:8)

2. I have declared, and have saved, and I have shewed. Therefore, ye are my witnesses, saith the Lord, that I am God. (43:12)

3. That confirmeth the word of his servant, and performeth the counsel of his messengers. (44:26)

4. Thus saith the Lord, Ask me of things to come concerning my sons, and concerning the work of my hands. (45:11)

5. I am God, declaring the end from the beginning, and the things that are not yet done. I have spoken it, I will also bring it to pass; I have proposed it, I will also do it. (46:9-11)

6. I have declared the former things from the beginning; and they went forth from my mouth, and I shewed them; before it came to pass I shewed it thee. (48:3-5)

7. Hear ye this; I have not spoken in secret from the beginning; from the time that it was, there am I; and now the Lord God, and his Spirit, hath sent me. (48:16)

45. God is a Rewarder of Good and Evil:
(2 Ki. 17:25; 21:14; 2 Chron. 13:12; Amos 9:2, 3, 4; Hos. 4:9*; 14:9; Is. 3:10; 13:11*; 48:22; 64:4; Nahum 1:3; Jer. 25:14; 32:19*; Lam. 1:5; 2:2; 3:64; Ezek. 7:3, 4, 27; 11:21; 14:23; 22:31; 24:14; 44:12-13; Zech. 1:6)

1. Say ye to the righteous, that it shall be well with him: for they shall eat the fruit of their doings. (13:10)

2. Woe unto the wicked! It shall be ill with him: for the reward of his hands shall be given him. (13:11)

3. There is no peace, saith the Lord, unto the wicked. (48:22)

4. Men have not heard, neither hath the eye seen, O God, beside thee, what he hath prepared for him that waiteth for him. (64:4)

46. God is Righteous:
(2 Chron. 19:7*; Hos. 14:9; Mic. 6:3-5*; 7:8-9; Is. 5:16; 16:5; 33:5; 45:19*; 46:13; 63:1; Jer. 4:2; 12:1; 9:24*; Lam. 1:18; Ezra 9:15; Dan. 9:7, 14; Neh. 9:8, 33; Zech. 8:8)

1. God that is holy shall be sanctified in righteousness. (5:16)

2. He shall sit upon the throne in truth, judging, and seeking judgment, and hasting righteousness. (16:5)

3. The Lord is exalted; he hath filled Zion with judgment and righteousness. (33:5)

4. I the Lord speak righteousness, I declare things that are right. (45:19)

5. I bring near my righteousness; it shall not be far off. (46:13)

6. I that speak righteousness, mighty to save. (63:1)

47. God Is Slow To Anger: (Jon. 4:2; Nahum 1:3; Neh. 9:17; Joel 2:13)

48. God Is the Source of Salvation:
(Jon. 2:9; Is. 45:17; Hab. 3:13)
    1. Israel shall be saved in the Lord with an everlasting salvation: ye shall not be ashamed nor confounded world without end. (45:17)

49. God Is the Source of Strength:
(Is. 41:10, 13; 49:5; Hab. 3:19; Joel 3:16)
    1. I will strengthen thee; yea, I will help thee. (41:10)

50. God Is a Stumbling Stone to the Wicked: (Is. 8:14-15)
    1. He shall be for a sanctuary; but for a stone of stumbling and for a rock of offence, for a gin and for a snare; and many among them shall stumble, and fall, and be broken, and be snared, and be taken. (8:14-15)

51. God Tests Men:
(2 Chron. 32:31; Is. 48:10; Zech. 13:9)
    1. Behold, I have refined thee, but not with silver; I have chosen thee in the furnace of affliction. (48:10)

52. God Requires True Religion: (Hos. 6:6; Mic. 6:6-8)

53. God Speaks Truth: (Is. 16:5; Jer. 4:2; 10:10; Zech. 8:8)
    1. In mercy shall the throne be established: and he shall sit upon it in truth. (16:5)

54. God is Unchangeable: (Mal. 3:6)

55. God Shows Visions to His Servants: (2 Ki. 2:11; 6:17; 13:14; Hab. 2:2-3; Ezek. 1:1, 4-25, 26-28; 3:23-24; 8:1-3; 8:4-11:24; Dan. 3:25; 5:5; 6:22; 7:13-14; 9:20-27; 10:5-7, 10-21)

56. God May be Weary: (Jer. 6:11)

57. God's Ways Differ From Man's:
(Hos. 11:9; Is. 55:8-9)
    1. My thoughts are not your thoughts, neither are your ways my ways, saith the Lord. For as the heavens are higher than the earth, so are my ways higher than your ways, and my thoughts than your thoughts. (55:8-9)

58. God Withdraws From Man Because of Man's Wickedness:

(Mic. 3:6-7; Is. 54:7, 8; 60:10; 63:10; 64:7; Jer. 7:16; 11:14; 14:11; 15:1; Ezek. 20:1-3, 31; 14:7-8)

1. For a small moment have I forsaken thee; in a little wrath I hid my face from thee for a moment. (54:7-8)

2. For in my wrath I smote thee. (60:10)

3. But they rebelled, and vexed his holy Spirit: therefore he was turned to be their enemy, and he fought against them. (63:10)

4. Thou hast hid thy face from us, and hast consumed us, because of our iniquities. (64:7)

An examination of the above outline reveals a God who is possessor of many attributes, many of which are the same attributes which he gave unto man in the creation. He may be regarded as a Being who knows and understands man's thoughts, feelings, and actions, and who is endowed with all the qualities one would hope to attain in his own quest for eventual perfection. God is man's pattern and model for growth.

> For the LORD will have mercy on Jacob, and will yet choose Israel, and set them in their own land: and the strangers shall be joined with them, and they shall cleave to the house of Jacob.
>
> And the people shall take them, and bring them to their place: and the house of Israel shall possess them in the land of the LORD for servants and handmaids: and they shall take them captives, whose captives they were; and they shall rule over their oppressors.
>
> (Isaiah 14:1-2)

10

GOD'S COMMUNICATION WITH MAN

The second of the major doctrines of the Old Testament prophets deals with the manner in which God manifests His will to mortals. To comprehend the method of God's communication with man, one must fully understand the functions of God's servants, the prophets. The Old Testament gives a comprehensive view of the manner in which prophets serve as spokesmen and agents for the Lord. In addition, it becomes clear that prophets and other individuals received revelation for their personal needs through the Holy Ghost.

The Prophetic Functions

1. Prophets are Spokesmen and Agents for God:
(1 Ki. 22:14, 28; 2 Ki. 3:11, 15; 17:13; 18:40; 21:10; 2 Chron. 18:13, 27; Jon. 1:2; 3:2; Hos. 12:10; 12:13; Is. 48:16; Jer. 1:7, 9, 17; 2:1; 3:15; 7:2; 11:2-3, 6; 19:1-2; 27:1-4; 22:1-2; 26:2; 7:25; 25:4, 13; 26:5; 28:9; Dan. 9:10)

1. Hear ye this: I have not spoken in secret from the beginning; from that time that it was, there am I; and now the Lord God, and his Spirit, hath sent me. (48:16)

2. Prophets are Witnesses for God: (2 Ki. 17:13; Amos 3:3-15; Neh. 9:30)

3. Prophets are Writers and Compilers of Revelation: (Hab. 2:2-3; Jer. 36:1-4, 27-32; 30:2; Dan. 7:1; 12:4, 9)

4. God Reveals His Mysteries to the Prophets:
(Amos 3:7; Is. 45:11; Jer. 33:3; Dan. 2:18-19, 20-22, 28, 45; 5:12)
 1. Thus saith the Lord: Ask me of things to come concerning my sons, and concerning the work of my hands command ye me. (45:11)

5. Prophets Are a Channel Through Which People May Inquire of the Lord:
(2 Ki. 3:11; Is. 45:11; Jer. 42:1-6; 21:2; 37:3; 37:17; 42:2; Ezek. 7:25-26)
 1. Thus saith the Lord: Ask me of things to come concerning my sons, and concerning the work of my hands command ye me. (45:11)

6. Prophets Must Speak the Lord's Will: (1 Ki. 22:14; 2 Chron. 18:13; Amos 3:6-8; Jer. 1:7, 9, 17; 2:1; 7:2; 22:1-2; 26:2*; 15:16; 17:16; 29:9*; Ezek. 33:1-8; 2:4; 3:26-27*)

7. God Chooses the Men Who are to be His Prophets:
(Amos 2:11; 7:14-15; Is. 6:8; Jer. 1:4-5; Ezek. 1, 2, 3)
 1. I heard the voice of the Lord, saying, Whom shall I send, and who will go for us? Then said I, Here am I; send me. (6:8)

8. Prophets and Prophecies Should be Verified by the Spirit of Discernment:
(1 Ki. 13:11-32; 22:6-28; 2 Chron. 18:5-27; Is. 44:26)
 1. That confirmeth the word of his servant, and performeth the counsel of his messengers. (44:26)

9. Fulfillment of His Prophecy is the Test of a Prophet: (1 Ki. 22:28; 2 Chron. 18:27; Jer. 28:6-9)

10. Prophets Receive Visions and Revelations from God: (Hos. 12:10; Dan. 2, 7, 8, 10-12; Ezek. 1-3, 8, 9, 10; Neh. 9:13-14)

The Nature of Revelation and Prophecy

11. Much Revelation Is Received Through the Holy Spirit:
(1 Ki. 18:12; 19:12; 2 Ki. 2:9, 16; 2 Chron. 15:1; 20:14; 24:20; Is. 11:2-3; 32:15; 42:5; 44:3; 63:11, 14; Ezek. 1:12, 20; 2:2; 3:12-14; 8:3; 11:1; 11:24; 11:4-5*; 37:1; Neh. 9:20; Hag. 1:14; 2:5; Joel 2:28-29; Zech. 4:6; 7:12)

1. And the spirit of the Lord shall rest upon him, the spirit of wisdom and understanding, the spirit of counsel and might, the spirit of knowledge and of the fear of the Lord; and shall make him of quick understanding in the fear of the Lord. (11:2-3)

2. Until the spirit be poured upon us from on high. (32:15)

3. Thus saith God the Lord, he that giveth breath unto the people upon it, and spirit to them that walk therein. (42:5)

4. I will pour my spirit upon thy seed, and my blessing upon thine off-spring. (44:3)

5. Where is he that put his holy Spirit within him? (63:11)

6. The Spirit of the Lord caused him to rest. (63:14)

12. Prophecy Serves to Prove the Lord Is God:
(Is. 44:26; 46:9-11; 48:3; 55:10-11; Hab. 2:2-3; Jer. 40:21; 42:9)

1. That confirmeth the word of his servant, and performeth the counsel of his messengers. (44:26)

2. I am God, declaring the end from the beginning. Yea, I have spoken it, I will also bring it to pass. (46:9-11)

3. I have declared the former things from the beginning; and went forth out of my mouth, and I shewed them. (48:3)

4. So shall my word be that goeth forth out of my mouth: it shall not return unto me void, but it shall accomplish that which I please, and it shall prosper in the thing whereto I sent it. (55:10-11)

13. The Lord Brings to Pass the Fulfillment of His Prophecies:
(2 Chron. 10:15; 36:21; 36:22-23; Is. 44:26; 46:9-11; 48:3; 55:10-11; Hab. 2:2-3; Jer. 25:13; 1:12; 25:13*; Lam. 2:17; Ezek. 33:30-33; 2:5; 5:13; 12:21-25*; Ezra 1:1; Neh. 9:8)

1. That confirmeth the word of his servant, and performeth the counsel of his messengers. (44:26)

2. I am God, declaring the end from the beginning. Yea, I have spoken it, I will also bring it to pass. (46:9-11)

3. I have declared the former things from the beginning; and they went forth out of my mouth, and I shewed them. (48:3)

4. So shall my word be that goeth forth out of my mouth: it shall not return unto me void, but it shall accomplish that which I please, and it shall prosper in the thing whereto I sent it. (55:10-11)

14. Prophecy Is Specific and Accurate and Receives Literal Fulfillment: (2 Ki. 10:10; 17:23; 24:2; *Examples:* 1 Ki. 11:29-12:20; 14:1-18 & 15:25-30; 1 Ki. 13:1-10 & 2 Ki. 23:1-18; 1 Ki. 13:11-32; 13:1-13; 19:1-21 & 2 Ki. 8:13-29 & 9:15-10:30 & 13:14-25; 1 Ki. 21:17-29 & 2 Ki. 9:22-10:11; 2 Chron. 21:12-20; 1 Ki. 20:13-21; 20:28-30; 20:31-43 & 22:34-38; 2 Chron. 20:14-30; 2 Ki. 6:24-7:20; 8:7-29; 9:1-10 & 9:22-10:11; 21:1-16)

15. Prophecy Is Not Predestination. When Situations Change, the Outcome of Prophecy May Change:
(2 Chron. 12:2-12; 1 Ki. 22:6-38; 2 Chron. 18:5-27; 25:1-12; 2 Ki. 22:13-23:30; 2 Chron. 34:22-28; Jon. 3:5-10; 4:10-11; Amos 7:1-3; 7:4-6; Is. 38)

1. The account of King Hezekiah's winning of 15 more years of life because of his righteous pleas to the Lord, who sent Isaiah with an altered instruction to the king. (38)

16. Man's Life Is Not Predestined. Man Himself Determines His Fate by Establishing in the Present a Cause-and-Effect Relationship With the Future. Prophecy Merely Pre-states What the Ultimate Effect of Present Actions Will Be: (2 Chron. 16:7-10; 2 Ki. 1:1-4; 1 Ki. 20:31-43; 1 Ki. 22:6-28; 2 Chron. 18:5-27; 2 Ki. 5:1-19; 2 Ki. 6:24-7:20; 13:14-21; 2 Chron. 25:1-12; 25:15-28)

In addition to the information above, the student of this topic should examine the following list of thirty-five lessons concerning the prophets and their calling, drawn from a chapter summary in the author's book, *Prophets and Prophecies of the Old Testament*, pp. 245-46:

1. God reveals the future to his prophets.
2. Prophecy is specific and accurate.
3. Prophecy is literally fulfilled.
4. God warns his prophets of approaching challenges and dangers.
5. God directs people, through his prophets, as to how they should conduct their lives.
6. God rules the destiny of nations.

7. God will not allow men to disturb his plans.

8. When situations change, the outcome of prophecy may change.

9. When God changes prophetic outcomes, he reveals the change to his prophet.

10. Man can avert or soften a prophecy of the Lord's punishment against him by truly repenting and manifesting humility.

11. A prophet can foresee events hundreds of years into the future, and in differing national situations.

12. God often shows the truthfulness of a prophecy be giving a sign which receives immediate fulfillment.

13. A prophet can call upon the powers of God to smite and curse his enemies.

14. A prophet can call upon the powers of God to heal and remove curses.

15. God demands that his prophets be treated with reverence and respect.

16. God can use a man as a prophet even though the man is not free from sin.

17. God demands strict obedience from his prophets.

18. Man should test the prophets and their prophecies by the spirit of discernment.

19. Revelation serves for commendation as well as reproof.

20. Man's life is not predestined. Man himself determines his fate by establishing in the present a cause-and-effect relationship with the future. Prophecy merely pre-states what the ultimate effect of present actions will be.

21. God often uses many prophets at the same time.

22. A calling as a prophet did not necessarily require that the person with this calling stand at the head of the church.

23. God gives his prophets control over nature to further his work.

24. God protects his prophets and supplies their needs.

25. Prophets have the power to perform miracles.

26. Some miracles are performed by the powers already vested in the prophet. For other miracles he must call upon God.

27. Miracles are often used to establish the divinity of Jehovah and the authority of his prophets.

28. On special occasions God gives his servants strength beyond the normal limits of endurance.

29. Many miracles are designed for the convenience of God's servants.

30. Some servants of God are transferred from this earth to another. They become translated beings.

31. Prophets have the power to discern the thoughts and deeds of others.

32. At times people perform specific actions to intentionally fulfill prophecies.

33. The Bible does not record the fulfillment of some prophecies. This does not, however, make them untrue.

34. At times prophets must suffer martyrdom for their testimony.

35. Women can also speak the Lord's will, as prophetesses.

The spirit of the Lord God is upon me; because the Lord hath anointed me to preach good tidings unto the meek; he hath sent me to bind up the brokenhearted, to proclaim liberty to the captives, and the opening of the prison to them that are bound;

To proclaim the acceptable year of the Lord, and the day of vengeance of our God; to comfort all that mourn;

(Isaiah 61:1-2)

11

THE NATURE OF SIN

To understand the third basic doctrine of the Old Testament prophets, the nature of sin, one must understand the plans and purpose of a wise and loving God. A fundamental principle in God's master plan of creation is that man is to progress and strive for perfection. Indeed, the ultimate objective of mortal life is for man to attain the perfection of immortality and eternal life.

There are forces and influences which aid man in approaching his goal. There are also certain actions and influences which retard man in his progress toward exaltation. God has seen fit to reveal unto man many keys which will help him to progress toward perfection. As one of these keys, He has indicated in detailed form the actions, attitudes, and thoughts which will retard man's progress toward his goal. When man does that which retards his progress, he does that which opposes God's plan. He does that which displeases God; he commits sin. Obstructions or hindrances to the progress of God's plan may be small or great, but they will always leave their mark upon man and those around him.

The nature of sin has remained constant. That which was wickedness in Old Testament times is still wickedness today. One of the most valuable contributions of the Old Testament is that it reveals to man the pitfalls which he should avoid. They are considered in this context as being divisible into five categories: 1. Perversion of religious truths and practices; 2. Apathy, lack of faith, and negative personal traits; 3. Rejection and opposition to God's plan; 4. Moral depravity, and 5. Social, economic and national wickedness.

As in the other chapters on the major doctrines of the Old Testament prophets, this chapter will list numerous references from the various prophetic books on the various subjects, but will summarize in detail the specific passages from the book of Isaiah which are pertinent to the topic. Again, passages which are considered to be especially pertinent are identified with an asterisk (*).

Perversions of Religious Truths and Practices

1. They Accept Corrupt Religious Leaders: (Mic. 3:11; Zeph. 3:4)

2. False Prophets and Precepts Lead People Astray:
(Mic. 3:5; Is. 29:13; 44:18, 20; Ezek. 13:2-4, 9, 22; 20:13, 16)
    1. This people draw near to me with their mouth, but have removed their heart far from me, and their fear toward me is taught by the precept of men. (29:13)
    2. They have not known or understood, he cannot deliver his soul. (44:18, 20)

3. Pagan Worship and Religious Harlotry is Practiced: (Amos 4:4-5; Hos. 1:2; 4:13-19; 5:1-3; 6:10)

4. They Practice Idolatry: (1 Ki. 11:7-8, 33; 14:9; 2 Ki. 17:7-12, 16; 21:3-7; Amos 5:26; Hos. 8:4; 9:10; 11:2; 13:1-2; Mic. 1:7; Zeph. 1:4-5; Hab. 2:19; Jer. 1:16; 2:13; Ezek. 8:12-16; 16:17-19; 23:27; 33:25; Dan. 5:23; Zech. 10:2)

5. The Pastors Transgress:
(Is. 43:27; Jer. 2:8; 10:21; 12:10-11; 23:1-2)
    1. Thy first father hath sinned, and thy teachers have transgressed against me. (43:27)

6. The Religious Leaders Err: (Zeph. 3:4; Jer. 2:8; 5:21; 7:9; 10:21; 12:10-11; 14:13-16; 20:6; 23:1-2, 11, 13, 16-17, 21-22, 25-40; 27:9-10, 14-18; 28:1-17; 29:8-9; Ezek. 13:2-4, 19; 22:26, 28; 34:2-4, 6, 8; Zech. 10:2; Mal. 2:8)

7. Enchantments, Familiar Spirits, Wizards are Sought: (2 Ki. 17:17; 21:6; 2 Chron. 33:6; Nahum 3:4)

8. The False Clergy Corrupts and Labors for Money: (Hos. 6:9; Mic. 3:11)

9. They Offer Human Sacrifices: (2 Ki. 16:3; 17:17; 21:6; 2 Chron. 28:2-4; 33:6; Jer. 7:21; 19:4-5; 32:35; Ezek. 16:20-21; 23:37)

10. They Break the Sabbath: (Ezek. 20:13, 16; 23:38)

11. They Serve Other Gods: (1 Ki. 11:4; 2 Ki. 17:7-8; Hab. 1:11; Jer. 1:16; 2:25-28; 7:9, 18-20; 13:10; 17:2; 18:15; 19:4-5; Ezek. 16:26-29)

Apathy, Lack of Faith, and Negative Personal Traits

12. They Have Apathy: (Amos 6:1; Zeph. 1:12; Mal. 1:13; 3:14)

13. They Do Not Know God: (Jer. 2:8; 4:22; 9:3)

14. They Do Not Seek God: (Hos. 7:10, 16; Zeph. 3:2; Jer. 2:8)

15. They Do Not Trust God: (Zeph. 3:2)

16. They are Doubters: (Is. 5:19)
   1. They say, Let him make speed, and hasten his work, that we may see it. (5:19)

17. They Have No Knowledge; No Understanding:
(Amos 3:10; Hos. 4:1, 6, 14; Is. 1:3; 5:13; 44:19; Obad. 7; Jer. 4:22; 5:21; 9:23-24)
   1. Israel doth not know, my people doth not consider. (1:3)
   2. My people are gone into captivity, because they have no knowledge. (5:13)
   3. None considereth in his heart, neither is there knowledge nor understanding. (44:19)

18. They Have No Mercy:
(Hos. 4:1; Is. 47:6; Obad. 14)
   1. Thou didst shew them no mercy; upon the ancient hast thou very heavily laid thy yoke. (47:6)

19. They are Not Valiant: (1 Ki. 11:6; Jer. 9:3; Mal. 1:13)

20. They Oppose Righteousness:
(2 Chron. 19:2; Amos 5:10; 6:12; Is. 5:23; Hab. 1:4; Jer. 11:21)
   1. Which justify the wicked for reward, and take away the righteousness of the righteous from him! (5:23)

21. They Have a Religion of Ritual Only:
(Amos 5:21-23; Hos. 7:14; Is. 1:10-14)
   1. Bring no more vain oblations; your new moons and your appointed feasts my soul hateth: they are a trouble unto me. (1:10-14)

22. They are Self-righteous and Self-justified:
(Is. 65:5; Jer. 7:10; Mal. 3:15)
    1. Which say, Stand by thyself, come not near to me. (65:5)

23. They Make Wrong Judgments:
(Amos 5:18-20; Mic. 3:11; Mal. 2:17; 3:15)

Rejection and Opposition To God's Plan

24. They Commit Blasphemy:
(Is. 52:5; Ezek. 20:27)
    1. My name continually every day is blasphemed. (52:5)

25. They Break God's Covenants and Laws:
(Hos. 6:7; 8:1; Is. 24:5; Jer. 11:10; 34:18; Ezek. 16:59)
    1. They have transgressed the laws, changed the ordinance, broken the everlasting covenant. (24:5)

26. They Defile and Desecrate: (Amos 2:8; Zeph. 3:4; Jer. 2:7; 3:9; 7:30; 32:34; Ezek. 5:11; 23:38; 28:18; 36:17)

27. They are Disobedient:
(1 Ki. 11:10; 2 Chron. 33:10; Hos. 7:13; Is. 42:24; Jer. 3:25; 9:13; 44:23; Ezek. 3:7; 11:12; 20:13, 16; Dan. 9:6, 10; Zech. 1:4; Mal. 3:7, 8)
    1. They walk not in his ways, neither were they obedient unto his law. (42:24)

28. They Have Forsaken God:
(1 Ki. 11:9, 33; 2 Ki. 17:9, 15, 16; 21:22; 2 Chron. 12:1; 29:6; Amos 4:6, 8, 9, 10, 11; Is. 1: 4*; 5:24*; 17:10; 43:22; 66:4; Jer. 1:16; 2:5; 13*, 31, 32; 3:17, 21; 5:7, 19; 9:13; 13:25; 32 :33)
    1. They have forsaken the Lord, they are gone away backward. (1:4)
    2. They have cast away the law of the Lord of hosts, and despised the word of the Holy One of Israel. (5:24)
    3. Thou hast forgotten the God of thy salvation, and hast not been mindful of the rock of thy strength. (17:10)
    4. Thou hast not called upon me, O Jacob; but thou hast been weary of me, O Israel. (43:22)
    5. When I called, none did answer; when I spake, they did not hear. (66:4)

29. They are Headstrong and Stubborn:
(Is. 66:3*; Jer. 18:18; 19:15; 22:21; 32:33*; 37:2; 44:10, 16, 23; 48:26, 27; Ezek. 2:4*)

1. They have chosen their own ways, and their soul delighteth in their abominations. (66:3)

30. Their Hearts are Not Right: (1 Ki. 11:4; 2 Chron. 12:14; 20:33; 25:2)

31. They are Irreverent: (Amos. 2:8; Ezek. 36:23; Dan. 5:23; Mal. 2:11)

32. They are Rebellious:
(2 Chron. 33:23; Hos. 7:14; Is. 1:2, 23; 3:8; 29:16; 65:2; Jer. 4:17; 8:6; 29:32; Ezek. 2:3; 5:6; 12:2; Dan. 5:22-23; 9:5; Zech. 7:11; Mal. 3:13)

1. They have rebelled against me. (1:2)
2. Thy princes are rebellious, and companions of thieves. (1:23)
3. Their tongue and their doings are against the Lord, to provoke the eyes of his glory. (3:8)
4. Shall the work say of him that made it, He made me not? (29:16)
5. I have spread out my hands unto a rebellious people, which walketh in a way that was not good, after their own thoughts. (65:2)

33. They Reject God and His Prophets: (Amos 2:12; Mic. 2:6; Zeph. 1:6)

34. They Scorn God's Servants: (2 Chron. 13:9; 36:16; Zeph. 1:6)

35. They Will Not Receive Correction:
(Amos 5:10; Is. 29:21; Zeph. 3:2; Jer. 5:3)

1. They make a man an offender for a word, and lay a snare for him that reproveth in the gate. (29:21)

Moral Depravity

36. They Commit Adultery: (Amos 2:7; Hos. 4:2; 5:7; 7:4; Ezek. 23:37)

37. They Eat Human Flesh: (Jer. 19:9)

38. They are Corrupters: (Is. 1:4; Zeph. 3:7; Jer. 6:28; Mal. 2:8)

1. Ah, sinful nation, children that are corrupters: they have forsaken the Lord. (1:4)

39. They are Covetous: (Mic. 2:2; Hab. 2:5, 9; Jer. 6:13; 22:17; Ezek. 33:31)

40. They are Deceitful: (2 Ki. 17:9; Is. 1:10-14; 5:20; 10:6; 29:15*; 47:10; 48:1; Jer. 5:27*; 6:13, 14; 7:9, 28; 8:5, 11; 9:3, 5, 6, 8*; 23:10, 14; 29:23; Ezek. 33:31)

1. When ye come to appear before me, who hath required this at your hand, to tread my courts? (1:10-14)

2. Woe unto them that call evil good and good evil. (5:20)

3. I will send him against an hypocritical nation. (10:6)

4. Woe unto them that seek deep to hid their counsel from the Lord, and their works are in the dark. (29:15)

5. Thou hast trusted in thy wickedness: thou hast said, None seeth me. (47:10)

6. They make mention of the God of Israel, but not in truth, nor in righteousness. (48:1)

41. They are Drunken:
(Hos. 7:14; Is. 5:11, 22; Hab. 2:5, 15-16)

1. Woe unto them that rise up early that they may follow strong drink; till wine inflame them! (5:11)

2. Woe unto them that are mighty to drink wine, and men of strength to mingle strong drink. (5:22)

42. They Make False Covenants: (Hos. 10:4)

43. They are Generally Evil:
(1 Ki. 21:20; 2 Ki. 17:17; Amos 5:7; Hos. 4:8; Mic. 2:1; 3:2; 7:2; Is. 1:4; 65:12; 66:4; Jer. 3:5; 6:10; 9:3, 5; 22:13, 17; 23:14; Ezek. 11:2)

1. Ah sinful nation, a people laden with iniquity, a seed of evildoers, children that are corrupters: they have forsaken the Lord. (1:4)

2. When I called, ye did not answer; when I spake, ye did not hear; but did evil before mine eyes. (65:12)

3. They did evil before mine eyes, and chose that in which I delighted not. (66:4)

44. They Wear Improper Dress. (Zeph. 1:8)

45. They Lie: (Hos. 4:2; 7:1; 11:12; Mic. 6:12; Nahum 3:1; Jer. 14:13-16; Ezek. 13:19; 22:28; 24:12)

46. They are Morally Depraved: (Nahum 3:4; Jer. 2:20; 3:1-6, 9; 5:8; 6:15; 8:11; 9:3; 13:27; 23:10, 14; 29:23; Ezek. 22:11; 33:26)

47. They Commit Murder: (2 Ki. 21:16; Hos. 4:2; 7:7; Jer. 4:31; 7:9; 22:17; Ezek. 7:23; 22:12)

48. They Have Not Truth: (Hos. 4:1)

49. They Commit Robbery and Steal: (Amos 3:9-10; Hos. 4:2; 7:1; Nahum 3:1; Obad. 13; Jer. 7:9; Ezek. 22:29; Mal. 3:8)

50. They are Shameless: (Zeph. 3:5; Jer. 6:15; 8:11)

51. They Spoil and Commit Violence: (Hab. 1:3; 2:8, 10; Ezek. 7:23)

52. They Swear: (Hos. 4:2)

Social, Economic, and National Wickedness

53. They Betray Trust: (Mic. 7:2, 5-6)

54. They Give and Accept Bribes:
(Amos 5:12; Mic. 3:11; 7:3-4; Is. 1:23; Ezek. 22:12)
   1. Every one loveth gifts, and followeth after rewards. (1:23)

55. They Employ Dishonest Business Practices: (Amos 8:6; Mic. 6:11; Ezek. 22:12)

56. They Follow Unwise Counsel: (1 Ki. 12:8, 13-14; 2 Chron. 10:8; 22:3)

57. They are Unpatriotic: (Amos 6:6)

58. They Live Luxuriously: (Amos 3:15; 6:4-6)

59. They Oppress the Poor and Just:
(Amos 2:6, 7; 4:1; 5:11, 12; 8:4, 6; Mic. 2:2, 9; 3:2-3; Is. 1:23; 3:15; 5:8; 10:2; Hab. 3:14; Ezek. 16:49; 22:29)
   1. They judge not the fatherless, neither doth the cause of the widow come unto them. (1:23)
   2. Ye beat my people to pieces, and grind the faces of the poor. (3:15)
   3. Woe unto them that join house to house, that lay field to field, till there be no place. (5:8)

4. To turn aside the needy from judgment, and to take away the right from the poor of my people, that widows may be their prey, and that they may rob the fatherless! (10:2)

60. They Pervert Justice:
(Is. 5:23; 10:2; 29:21; Hab. 1:4; Jer. 5:28; Ezek. 5:6)
1. Which justify the wicked for reward, and take away the righteousness of the righteous from him! (5:23)
2. To turn aside the needy from judgment, and to take away the right from the poor of my people. (10:2)
3. That make a man an offender for a word, and lay a snare for him that reproveth in the gate, and turn aside the just for a thing of nought. (29:21)

61. The Political Leaders Err: (Jer. 2:8; 5:28; Ezek. 22:27; 28:2-6)

62. They Practice Slavery: (Jer. 34:11-16)

63. They Have Undeserved Pride: (Obad. 3, 12; Jer. 48:29; 49:16; Ezek. 16:49; 28:2-6, 17)

64. They Practice Racial Intermarriage: (Hos. 7:8-9; Mal. 2:11)

65. They Rule Unrighteously:
(Is. 3:12; 10:1; Ezek. 34:4)
1. They which lead thee cause thee to err, and destroy the way of thy paths. (3:12)
2. Woe unto them that decree unrighteous decrees, and that write grievousness which they have prescribed. (10:1)

66. They Set Up Kings Without Divine Approval: (Hos. 8:4)

67. They Slander: (Jer. 6:28)

68. They Seek Foreign Alliances Instead of Relying Upon God:
(Hos. 5:13; 7:11; 8:9-10; 9:3; 12:1; Is. 8:9-12)
1. Associate yourselves, O ye people, and ye shall be broken in pieces. Say ye not, A confederacy. (8:9-12)

69. They Cause Strife and Contention: (Hab. 1:3)

70. They Practice Treachery:
(Is. 24:16; Jer. 3:20; 5:11, 26, 27; 6:13; 9:8; Mal. 2:10)
1. The treacherous dealers have dealt very treacherously. (24:16)

71. They are Vain:

(Is. 5:18, 21; 10:13; 47:10; Zech. 10:2)

1. Woe unto them that draw iniquity with cords of vanity, and sin. (5:18)

2. Woe unto them that are wise in their own eyes, and prudent in their own sight! (5:21)

3. He saith, By the strength of my hand I have done it, and by my wisdom, for I am prudent. (10:13)

4. Thy wisdom and thy knowledge, it hath perverted thee; and thou hast said, I am, and none else beside me. (47:10)

72. They are Worldly Minded:

(Is. 3:16; 5:12; 47:8; Jer. 13:10; 48:7; Ezek. 16:15)

1. The daughters of Zion are haughty, with stretched forth necks, wanton eyes, walking and mincing as they go, and making a tinkling with their feet. (3:16)

2. They regard not the work of the Lord, neither consider the work of his hands. (5:12)

3. Thou art given to pleasures, dwellest carelessly. (47:8)

Each of the above items is regarded as sin in the scriptures. Each of them was displeasing in the eyes of God. Each of them will similarly retard man's progress and be displeasing to God if practiced today.

Depart ye, depart ye, go ye out from thence, touch no unclean thing; go ye out of the midst of her; be ye clean, that bear the vessels of the LORD.

(Isaiah 52:11)

12

THE NATURE OF MAN'S AGENCY AND GOD'S JUDGMENT

A fourth major doctrinal area of the Old Testament prophets concerns man's agency in relationship to God's eternal plan. The message of the Old Testament is that man has a sizeable degree of free agency. It appears, however, that God still maintains ultimate control of the fate of man, both individually and collectively. Man is given the freedom to choose his course in most situations, but God sometimes controls the choices which are available to him.

Man has the agency to control his own relationship with God through obedience or disobedience to divine commandments. Thus, he partially controls his fate. Actions and attitudes have a result, and God reveals Himself as the controller of future outcomes which are predicated on man's past and present activities and attitudes.

The relationship between God and man appears to be very similar to that of a mortal parent with his young children. The parent gives the children choices and responsibilities to help them grow, but controls the limits, scope, and nature of their activities. In this way the activities function in the best interests of the children and operate in conformity with parental plans and objectives.

Divine reward and punishment is just. Many rewards or punishments, however, come as the direct result of righteousness or sin, and are not sent from God. As in the other chapters, references on many aspects of agency and judgment are listed from all the Old Testament prophets. Those from Isaiah are specifically listed in summary form. Passages judged to be especially significant are identified with an asterisk (*).

Man and His Agency

1. Man is a Free Agent and Makes His Choices:
(2 Chron. 13:12; 15:2*; 24:20; Amos 5:1-9; Is. 1:18-20; Jer. 21:8*; Lam. 3:27-41; Mal. 2:2)

1. If ye be willing and obedient, ye shall eat the good of the land: But if ye refuse and rebel, ye shall be devoured with the sword. (1:18-20)

2. Man's Life is Not Predestined. Man Himself Determines His Fate By Establishing in the Present a Cause-and-Effect Relationship With the Future. Prophecy Merely Pre-states What the Ultimate Effect of Present Actions Will Be: (2 Chron. 16:7-10; 2 Ki. 1:1-4; 1 Ki. 20:21-43; 1 Ki. 22:6-28; 2 Chron. 18:5-27; 2 Ki. 5:1-19; 2 Ki. 6:24-7:20; 13:14-21; 2 Chron. 25:1-12; 25:15-28)

3. Man's Attitude Toward God Influences God's Attitude Toward Man: (2 Chron. 24:20; Hos. 4:6; Zech. 1:3, 15; 7:12, 13)

God's Interactions with Man's Agency

4. God Tests Man:
(2 Chron. 32:31; Is. 48:10; Zech. 13:9)

1. I have refined thee, but not with silver; I have chosen thee in the furnace of affliction. (48:10)

5. God Knows Man's Thoughts and Acts:
(2 Ki. 19:27; 2 Chron. 16:9*; Jon. 1:2; 3:10; Amos 4:13; 5:12*; 8:7; 9:8; Mic. 1:2; Is. 37:28*; 66:18; Nahum 1:7; Jer. 2:1, 34; 5:3; 12:3; 16:17*; 17:10; 21:10; 23:24; 29:23; 32:19*; Zech. 4:10)

1. I know thy abode, and thy going out, and thy coming in, and thy rage against me. (37:28)

2. I know their works and their thoughts. (66:18)

6. God Both Rewards and Punishes:
(2 Ki. 17:25; 21:14; 2 Chron. 13:12; Amos 9:2, 3, 4; Hos. 4:9*; 14:9; Is. 3:10; 13:11*; 48:22; 64:4; Nahum 1:3; Jer. 25:14; 32:19*; Lam. 1:5; 2:2; 3:64; Ezek. 3:18-21; 7:2, 4, 27; 11:21; 14:23; 18:21-29; 22:31; 24:14; 33:12-20; 44:12-13; Zech. 1:6)

1. Say unto the righteous, that it shall be well with him: for they shall eat the fruit of their doings. (3:10)

2. I will punish the world for their evil, and the wicked for their iniquity. (13:11)

3. There is no peace, saith the Lord, unto the wicked. (48:22)

4. Men have not heard, nor perceived by the ear, neither hath the eye seen, O God, beside thee, what he hath prepared for him that waiteth for him. (64:4)

7. Man is Judged for His Own Deeds:
(Is. 3:10; 5:15; 13:11*; Jer. 2:19; 17:10; 21:14; 25:14; 31:30; 48:10; Ezek. 18:20*; Zech. 1:6)

1. Say unto the righteous, that it shall be well with him: for they shall eat the fruit of their doings. (3:10)

2. The mean man shall be brought down, and the mighty man shall be humbled, and the eyes of the lofty shall be humbled. (5:15)

3. I will punish the world for their evil, and the wicked for their iniquity; and I will cause the arrogancy of the proud to cease, and will lay low the haughtiness of the terrible. (13:11)

8. Punishment is the Result of Sin:
(2 Ki. 17:25; 2 Chron. 21:14; 36:16; Is. 3:9-11; 13:11; Jer. 2:19; 5:25; 14:7; 17:11; 20:4; 23:36)

1. Woe unto the wicked! It shall be ill with him: for the reward of his hands shall be given him. (3:9-11)

2. I will punish the world for their evil, and the wicked for their iniquity; and I will cause the arrogancy of the proud to cease, and will lay low the haughtiness of the terrible. (13:11)

9. Punishment May Be Avoided or Softened Through Repentance:
(2 Chron. 12:7*, 12; 19:2-11; 32:26; 33:11-13; 34:27-28; 1 Ki. 21:17-29; Jer. 18:7-10; 26:13; 31:34; 33:8; Ezek. 18:20-22*; 33:8-20)

10. Punishment is Certain in the Absence of Repentance:
(Is. 50:1; Jer. 1:16; 2:22; 4:12; 5:3, 4; 6:19; 14:10, 16; 15:7; 16:18-21; 17:18; 22:22; 44:29; 51:56; Ezek. 7:27; 11:21; 14:23; 22:31; 24:14; 44:12-13; Zech. 1:6)

1. For your iniquities have ye sold yourselves, and for your transgressions is your mother put away. (50:1)

11. God Withdraws His Spirit From the Wicked:
(Mic. 3:6-7; Is. 54:7-8; 60:10; 63:10; 64:7; Jer. 7:16; 11:14; 14:11; 15:1; Ezek. 14:7-11; 20:1-3, 31; Mal. 1:10)

1. For a small moment have I forsaken thee; in a little wrath I hid my face from thee for a moment. (54:7-8)

2. For in my wrath I smote thee. (60:10)

3. But they rebelled, and vexed his holy Spirit. (63:10)

4. Thou hast hid thy face from us, and hast consumed us, because of our iniquities. (64:7)

Kinds of Punishment Specified by the Old Testament Prophets

1. Captivity: (Amos 5:5, 27; 7:11; Mic. 4:8-10)

2. Chastisement: (Hos. 7:12; 8:7; 9:6; 10:8; Mic. 6:16)

3. Death (various circumstances): (Amos 6:9-10; 7:17; 8:3, 14; Hos. 10:14)

4. Destruction, desolation, loss of lands:
(Amos 1:2; 3:11, 14, 15; 5:5; 6:10; 7:9, 17; 9:8; Hos. 4:5-6, 14; 5:9; 8:14; 9:2, 12; 10:8; Mic. 1:6, 7; 3:12; 6:16; Is. 1:7; 7:23-25; 8:4)

1. Your country is desolate, your cities are burned with fire: your land, strangers devour it in your presence, and it is desolate. (1:7)

2. With arrows and bows shall men come thither; because all the land shall become briers and thorns. (7:23-25)

3. The riches of Damascus and the spoil of Samaria shall be taken away before the king of Assyria. (8:4)

5. Elements to be Disturbed: (Amos 8:9; 9:5)

6. Famine and Starvation: (Amos 4:6; Hos. 4:10; 8:7; 9:2; Mic. 6:14)

7. Glory To Diminish: (Hos. 9:11)

8. Lord's Name Is Forbidden: (Amos 6:10)

9. Nation Shall Fall:
(Hos. 1:4, 5; 10:15; Is. 7:8)

1. Within threescore and five years shall Ephriam be broken, that it be not a people. (7:8)

10. Nations Shall Afflict: (Amos 6:14)

11. No Increase: (Hos. 4:10; 9:14, 16)

12. Removal and Scattering:
(Amos 3:12; 4:2; 6:2-3; 9:9; Hos. 1:6; 8:3; 9:3, 17; Is. 3:1-3)
    1. The Lord of hosts doth take away from Jerusalem the mighty man, the judge, the prophet, the prudent, and the ancient, the captain, the counsellor, and the eloquent orator. (3:1-3)

13. Shame: (Hos. 4:7, 19; 10:6)

14. Sickness: (Mic. 6:13)

15. Sorrow and Mourning: (Amos 1:2; 5:16-17; 8:3, 10; Hos. 2:11; 4:3; 8:10)

16. Thirst: (Amos 8:13; Hos. 2:3)

17. Uncertain Crops: (Amos 4:7-10; Hos. 2:12; 8:7; Mic. 6:15; Hag. 1:10)

18. War:
(Amos 7:9, 11, 17; Hos. 7:16; 8:3; 11:6; Mic. 6:1; 6:14; Is. 3:25; 7:20; 8:7-8; 10:5-6)
    1. Thy men shall fall by the sword, and thy mighty in the war. (3:25)
    2. In the same day the Lord shall shave with a razor that is hired, the king of Assyria. (7:20)
    3. He shall pass through Judah; he shall overflow and go over, and fill the breadth of thy land. (8:7-8)
    4. O Assyrian, the rod of mine anger, I will send him against an hypocritical nation; I will give him a charge, to take a spoil, and to take the prey, and to tread them down. (10:5-6)

19. Weakness: (Amos 2:14-16)

20. Withdrawal of God:
(Amos 8:2, 11-12; Hos. 4:6; 5:6, 15; 9:15; Mic. 2:6; 3:4, 6-7; Is. 1:15; Ezek. 20:1-3. 31; Mal. 1:10)
    1. I will hide mine eyes from you: when ye make many prayers, I will not hear. (1:15)

21. Other Chastisements:
(Amos 9:1-4; 7:17; Is. 1:6; 3:4, 17-24; Hag. 2:17; Mal. 2:2)
    1. From the sole of the foot even unto the head there is no soundness in it; but wounds, and bruises, and putrifying sores. (1:6)
    2. I will give children to be their princes, and babes shall rule over them. (3:4)

3. In that day the Lord will take away the beauty, instead of sweet smell there shall be stink, baldness, a girding of sackcloth, and burning instead of beauty. (3:17-24)

God Controls Individuals, Their Actions and Their Fates

1. God Controls the Actions and Fate of Individuals:
(1 Ki. 11:14, 31, 34*, 36; 12:15; 20:42; 22:20-23; 2 Ki. 3:10*; 9:7; 10:30; 15:5, 12; 19:7; 24:20; 2 Chron. 10:15; 11:4; 13:20; 15:6-7; 16:7, 8; 18:31; 21:18; 25:16, 20; 26:16-20; 28:19; 33:11; 36:22; Mic. 7:8-9; Is. 29:10; 63:17; Ezek. 24:16-18; Ezra 7:6; Dan. 1:9, 17; 2:37; 4:17, 25, 32; Zech. 8:10)

1. The Lord hath poured out upon you the spirit of deep sleep, and hath closed your eyes; the prophets and your rulers, the seers hath he covered. (29:10)

2. O Lord, why hast thou made us to err from thy ways, and hardened our heart from thy fear? (63:17)

God Controls the Nations

1. God Controls the Actions and Fate of Nations:
(1 Ki. 12:24; 14:14; 20:13, 28; 2 Ki. 3:18; 8:19; 10:32; 13:5; 15:37*; 17:21)*; 19:34; 21:14; 24:2*, 3*; 2 Chron. 13:15-16*; 20:6-7, 27; 24:24*; 29:8; 30:12; 32:21; 36:17; Mic. 1:6; Is. 3:1-3; 7:20; Obad. 2, 4, 8; Jer. 5:15-17; 6:8; 7:3-7; 12:12, 17; 14:12; 15:4; 19:7; 20:5; 21:4-6, 7*; 25:9, 12; 27:8; 22:7; 32:3; 46:26; Ezek. 20:18-26; 29:19; 30:23-24; 38:16; 39:1-2; Dan. 1:1-2; 2:21)

1. The Lord doth take away from Jerusalem and from Judah the whole stay of bread and the whole stay of water; the mighty man, the judge, the prophet, the captain, the honourable man, and the counsellor. (3:1-3)

2. The Lord shall shave with a razor that is hired, the king of Assyria. (7:20)

The scriptures teach, as is illustrated above, that God gives man his personal free agency, but he also interacts with man in the exercise of that agency, and ultimately controls man's actions and fate. In the larger sense, God controls that actions and fates of nations. God both rewards and punishes, extending to man a broad range of blessings and a wide range of punishments. Man ultimately reaps the rewards of the seeds he sows: his thoughts, choices and actions.

13

COUNSEL FOR RIGHTEOUS LIVING

The fifth of the major doctrines of the Old Testament prophets is a treatment of God's program to aid man in living righteously. Throughout the scriptures one encounters a continual flow of precepts and examples which can guide man in his search for perfection. They are immediately applicable to man in his present circumstances, and they form the basis for man's righteous living. The prophetic section of the Old Testament is especially rich in such counsel and examples.

Listed in this chapter are key passages from the book of Isaiah on 14 important subjects. The passages are given in summary form.

1. Accept Counsel:
1. Take counsel, execute judgment. (Is. 16:3)

2. Aid the Afflicted and Oppressed, Help Others:
1. Learn to do well; seek judgment, relieve the oppressed, judge the fatherless, plead for the widow. (1:17)
2. Comfort ye my people, saith your God. (40:1)
3. The Lord hath given me the tongue of the learned, that I should know how to speak a word in season to him that is weary. (50:4)

3. Be Courageous and Strong:
1. Take heed, and be quiet; fear not, neither be fainthearted. (7:4)
2. Let him take hold of my strength, that he may make peace with me; and he shall make peace with me. (27:5)

3. Strengthen ye the weak hands, and confirm the feeble knees. Say to them that are of a fearful heart, Be strong, fear not. (35:3-4)

4. Lift up thy voice with strength; lift it up, be not afraid. (40:9)

5. They that waiteth upon the Lord shall renew their strength; they shall run, and not be weary; and they shall walk, and not faint. (40:31)

6. Fear not, for I am with thee: be not dismayed; for I am thy God: I will strengthen thee and help thee and uphold thee with the right hand of my righteousness. (41:10, 13)

7. My God shall be my strength. (49:5)

4. Be Humble:

1. The meek shall increase their joy in the Lord. (29:19)

2. To this man will I look, even to him that is poor and of a contrite spirit, and trembleth at my word. (66:2)

5. Do What Is Right:

1. With righteousness shall he judge the poor, and reprove with equity for the meek of the earth. (Is. 11:4)

2. Righteousness shall be the girdle of his loins, and faithfulness the girdle of his reins. (Is. 11:5)

3. The way of the just is uprightness: thou, most upright, dost weigh the path of the just. (Is. 26:7)

4. The work of righteousness shall be peace; and the effect of righteousness quietness and assurance for ever. (Is. 32:17)

5. Who shall dwell with everlasting burnings? He that walketh righteously, and speaketh uprightly; he that despiseth the gain of oppressions; that shaketh his hands from holding of bribes, that stoppeth his ears from hearing of blood, and shutteth his eyes from seeing evil, he shall dwell on high. (Is. 33:14-16)

6. (Hezekiah's prayer) Remember now, O Lord, I beseech thee, how I have walked before thee in truth and with a perfect heart, and have done that which is good in thy sight. (38:3)

7. All ye that kindle a fire, that compass yourselves about with sparks: walk in the light of the fire, and in the sparks that ye have kindled. (50:11)

8. In righteousness shalt thou be established. (54:14)

9. This is the heritage of the servants of the Lord, and their righteousness is of me, saith the Lord. (54:17)

6. Fear and Acknowledge God:

1. I will not ask, neither will I tempt the Lord. (7:12)

2. It is a small thing for you to weary men, but will ye weary my God also? (7:13)

3. Sanctify the Lord of hosts himself; and let him be your fear, and let him be your dread, and he shall be for a sanctuary. (8:13-14)

5. Shall the axe boast itself against him that heweth therewith? (10:15)

6. With righteousness shall he judge the poor, and reprove with equity for the meek of the earth. (11:4)

7. Righteousness shall be the girdle of his loins, and faithfulness the girdle of his reins. (11:5)

8. The way of the just is uprightness: thou, most upright, dost weigh the path of the just. (26:7)

9. The work of righteousness shall be peace; and the effect of righteousness quietness and assurance for ever. (32:17)

10. Who shall dwell with everlasting burnings? He that walketh righteously, and speaketh uprightly; he that despiseth the gain of oppressions; that shaketh his hands from holding of bribes, that stoppeth his ears from hearing of blood, and shutteth his eyes from seeing evil, he shall dwell on high. (33:14-16)

7. Gain Knowledge:

1. Learn to do well; seek judgment, relieve the oppressed, judge the fatherless, plead for the widow. (1:17)

2. Come now, and let us reason together, saith the Lord. (1:18)

3. He will teach us of his ways, and we will walk in his paths. (2:3)

4. Bind up the testimony, seal the law among my disciples. (8:16)

5. To the law and to the testimony: if they speak not according to this word, it is because there is no light in them. (8:20)

6. They that erred in spirit shall come to understanding, and they that murmured shall learn doctrine. (29:24)

7. Wisdom and knowledge shall be the stability of thy times, and strength of salvation: the fear of the Lord is his treasure. (33:6)

8. Seek ye out of the book of the Lord, and read. (34:16)

9. The Lord God hath given me the tongue of the learned, that I should know how to speak a word in season to him that is weary. (50:4)

10. That which they had not heard shall they consider. (52:15)

8. Give Glory to God:

1. With joy shall ye draw water out of the wells of salvation. (12:3)

2. Praise the Lord, call upon his name, declare his doings among the people, make mention that his name is exalted. (12:4)

3. Sing unto the Lord; for he hath done excellent things. (12:5)

4. O Lord, thou art my God, I will exalt thee, I will praise thy name. (25:1)

5. Sing unto the Lord a new song, and his praise from the end of the earth. (42:10-12)

6. I will greatly rejoice in the Lord, my soul shall be joyful in my God; for he hath clothed me with the garments of salvation, he hath covered me with the robe of righteousness. (61:10)

7. Be ye glad and rejoice for ever in that which the Lord creates. (65:18)

9. Have Faith:

1. Take heed, and be quiet, fear not, neither be fainthearted. (7:4)

2. If ye will not believe, surely ye shall not be established. (7:9)

3. I will not ask, neither will I tempt the Lord. (7:12)

4. Behold, God is my salvation; I will trust and not be afraid: for the Lord Jehovah is my strength and my song; he also is become my salvation. (12:2)

5. The Lord hath founded Zion, and the poor of his people shall trust in it. (14:32)

6. Thou wilt keep him in perfect peace, whose mind is stayed on thee: because he trusteth in thee. (26:3)

7. Trust ye in the Lord for ever: for in the Lord Jehovah is everlasting strength. (26:4)

8. Good is the word of the Lord which thou hast spoken. For there shall be peace and truth in my days. (39:8)

9. My God shall be my strength. (49:5)

10. Who is among you that feareth the Lord, that obeyeth the voice of his servant, that walketh in darkness, and hath no light? Let him trust in the name of the Lord, and stay upon his God. (50:10)

10. Learn of God and Seek Him:

1. He will teach us of his ways, and we will walk in his paths. (2:3)

2. I will wait upon the Lord, and I will look for him. (8:17)

3. Should not a people seek unto their God? for the living to the dead? (8:19)

4. The desire of our soul is to thy name, and to the remembrance of thee. (26:8)

5. With my soul have I desired thee in the night; yea, with my spirit within me will I seek thee early. (26:9)

6. Ye are my witnesses, saith the Lord, and my servant whom I have chosen that ye may know and believe me and understand that I am he. (43:10; 44:8)

7. Surely, shall one say, in the Lord have I righteousness and strength: even to him shall men come. (45:24)

8. Thou shalt know that I am the Lord: for they shall not be ashamed that wait for me. (49:23)

9. Hearken to me, ye that follow after righteousness, ye that seek the Lord. (51:1)

10. Hearken unto me, my people; and give ear unto me, O my nation. (51:4)

11. Wherefore do ye spend money for that which is not bread? and your labour for that which satisfieth not? hearken diligently to me, and eat ye that which is good. (55:2)

12. Incline your ear, and come unto me: hear, and your soul shall live. (55:3)

13. Seek ye the Lord while he may be found, call ye upon him while he is near. (55:6)

11. Prepare the Heart:

1. (Hezekiah's prayer) Remember now, O Lord, I beseech thee, how I have walked before thee in truth and with a perfect heart, and have done that which is good in thy sight. (38:3)

12. Repent:

1. Wash you, make you clean; put away the evil of your doings from before mine eyes; cease to do evil. (1:16)

2. Let the wicked forsake his way, and the unrighteous man his thoughts: and let him return unto the Lord, and he will have mercy upon him; and to our God, for he will abundantly pardon. (55:7)

13. Serve and Obey God:

1. He will teach us of his ways, and we will walk in his paths. (2:3)

2. Come ye, and let us walk in the light of the Lord. (2:5)

3. See ye, when he lifteth up an ensign on the mountains; and when he bloweth a trumpet, hear ye. (18:3)

4. Lord, thou wilt ordain peace for us: for thou also hast wrought all our works in us. (26:12)

5. O that thou hadst hearkened to my commandments! then had thy peace been as a river, and thy righteousness as the waves of the sea. (48:18)

6. Surely my judgment is with the Lord, and my work with my God. (49:4)

7. For Zion's sake will I not hold my peace, and for Jerusalem's sake I will not rest, until the righteousness thereof go forth as brightness, and the salvation thereof as a lamp that burneth. (62:1)

8. He who blesseth himself in the earth shall bless himself in the God of truth; and he that sweareth in the earth shall swear by the God of truth. (65:16)

9. All flesh shall come to worship before me. (66:23)

14. Teach and Warn Others:

1. Praise the Lord, call upon his name, declare his doings among the people, make mention that his name is exalted. (12:4)

2. The father to the children shall make known thy truth. (38:19)

3. Lift up thy voice with strength; lift it up, be not afraid. (40:9)

4. The Lord God hath given me the tongue of the learned, that I should know how to speak a word in season to him that is weary. (50:4)

5. How beautiful upon the mountains are the feet of him that bringeth good tidings of good, that publisheth salvation; that saith unto Zion, Thy God reigneth. (52:7)

6. All thy children shall be taught of the Lord; and great shall be the peace of thy children. (54:13)

7. Ye that make mention of the Lord, keep not silence. (62:6)

Therefore saith the Lord, the LORD of hosts, the mighty One of Israel, Ah, I will ease me of mine adversaries, and avenge me of mine enemies:

And I will turn my hand upon thee, and purely purge away thy dross, and take away all thy tin:

And I will restore thy judges as at the first, and thy counsellors as at the beginning: afterward thou shalt be called, The city of righteousness, the faithful city.

Zion shall be redeemed with judgment, and her converts with righteousness.

(Isaiah 1:24-27)

14

THE EVENTS OF THE LAST DAYS

The sixth major theme, the Lord's plan for His children in the last days, is undoubtedly the most predominant theme of the scriptures of the Church. Far more has even been said in them on this subject than concerning other such fundamental principles as faith, repentance, baptism, Church organization, etc. There can be little doubt that the Lord intends for man to understand His last-days program and to recognize the significance of coming events as they transpire.

The prophetic portion of the Old Testament makes an important contribution to the Church's understanding of future events. Indeed, it provides the nucleus around which the other prophecies center. Without understanding the Old Testament prophecies of the last days, one cannot hope to clearly envision the events of the future.

In other works[1] the author has attempted to compile prophetic evidence of the Savior's program for the last days and to determine a proper chronology for these events. In those volumes extensive evidence is cited to verify the conclusions determined therein. Those conclusions are not reported as an indication of the author's personal views, but rather as a composite picture of the message of the scriptures and of the prophets of the Church in the latter days. The evidence reported in those studies will not be repeated here. Instead, the reader is invited to consider a predetermined list of fifty important events which prophecy indicates are to take place in the last days.

_____
[1] See *Prophecy—Key to the Future*, which is based on a Master's Thesis written by the author in the College of Religious Instruction at the Brigham Young University. The thesis was prepared in fulfillment of the assignment to prepare and document a chronology of the future, listing major last-days events from the present to the end of the world, as found in the scriptures and statements of General Authorities of The Church of Jesus Christ of Latter-day Saints. Further last-days insights are found in other works by the author, including *Inspired Prophetic Warnings, The Prophecies of Joseph Smith*, and *Prophets and Prophecies of the Old Testament*.

With this list as an outline, the pertinent scriptural passages of the prophetic section of the Old Testament will be considered. It will be noted that some of the prophesied events will show few or no Old Testament references. They are documented from prophecies found in other of the four standard works or in prophecies of LDS General Authorities. They are listed and included in this context, however, because it would be impossible to understand the ordering of last days events without giving them proper consideration.

A listing and allocation of scriptures such as is being presented here of necessity involves considerable interpretation. The author is aware that there are people of other faiths who might disagree with the interpretations given for two reasons: (1) they may regard these Biblical passages as being uninspired, and therefore not applicable as a pattern for the future, or (2) they may regard them as prophecies which were fulfilled in the days of their prophets. Being a Latter-day Saint, the author feels willingly compelled to regard the scriptures from the same general viewpoint as the leaders of his Church, with the same eschatological direction as that which is expressed in the tenth Article of Faith: "We believe in the literal gathering of Israel and in the restoration of the Ten Tribes; that Zion (the New Jerusalem) will be built upon the American continent; that Christ will reign personally upon the earth; and, that the earth will be renewed and receive its paradisiacal glory."

Several factors should be kept clearly in mind while considering a list such as this one. *First*, extreme difficulty exists in showing the continuation of time in any list, and this list is no exception. The list indicates when continuing processes begin, but the reader must be alert to determine when some processes end. The proper interpretation of many passages is dependent on the chronological setting of the events they report. *Second*, many prophecies are so general that they cannot be connected to only one event. Thus the reader will find them cited under several topic headings where they may prove applicable. *Third*, some passages may be open to other lines of interpretation. An attempt will be made to distinguish such passages by placing a question mark after the quotation. It is deemed valuable to have all such passages listed, as an invitation to consideration, however, and so some passages which are subject to varying interpretations are indicated on the list. *Fourth*, it should be noted that many passages which have been posted to the list do not stand by themselves, but must be understood in the light of their context. The reader should investigate the context thoroughly with all such passages. *Fifth*, some passages are merely allusions to future events. While they carry little importance in and of themselves, they are significant because they contribute their weight to the pattern of scripture pertaining to the subject and indicate that the prophet was conversant with the coming event.

This listing is a beginning study guide. It is certainly not the final word that will be set forth on this important subject. The list is prepared in anticipation that new areas of contemplation may be opened to those who are interested in the field of Old Testament study. An in-depth coverage of the various events is provided in the author's book, *Prophecy—Key to the Future*. A complete listing of the 50 events, with passages from all the Old Testament prophets posted to the list, is found in the author's book, *Prophets and Prophecies of the Old Testament*.

It will be noted that the prophesied events tend to fall into two groups. The earlier events in the prophesied list occur primarily in the Americas. There is relatively little Biblical support for these events—most of the information comes from modern scriptures and the statements of General Authorities. The latter events in the prophesied list occur mainly in the Middle East or in Europe. Much of the prophetic information concerning these events is found in the Bible.

The 50-event list provides an overall view. When passages from the book of Isaiah are pertinent to a specific event, they are listed below the event's introduction and summary in the chapter order in which they appear in the book of Isaiah. If no Isaiah passages are listed, it is an indication that the prophesied event is based on revealed information from other sources.

1st Event: The Apostasy.

Latter-day Saints generally regard the apostasy as having begun during the time of the apostles in the first centuries A.D. With the end of that generation the apostasy became complete and continued until the restoration of the Church in 1830. In reality, the apostasy still continues among many people of the world and will extend in part to the end of the millennium. (See 1 Tim. 4:1-3; 2 Tim. 4:3-4; 2 Thess. 2:1-4; Gal. 1:6-8)

1. The Lord hath covered your prophets and seers. (29:9-10; see 2 Ne. 27:4-5, Morm. 1:13-19)

2nd Event: The Coming Forth of the Book of Mormon.

The Book of Mormon was revealed, translated, and published between 1823 and 1830. This section also contains prophetic references pertaining to the content of that book. (See JS–Hist. 1:30-75; D & C 2; 3; 5; 6; 8; 9; 10; 17)

1. The fall of the Nephites. Thou shalt speak out of the ground. Thy voice shall be as one that hath a familiar spirit. (29:1-4; See 2 Ne. 26:14-18; 30:4-6; Morm. 6:1-15)

2. The vision of all is become unto you as the words of a book that is sealed. (29:11)

3. The words of the book shall be delivered to one that is learned, saying, Read this, I pray thee: and he saith I cannot, for it is sealed. (29:11-12; See 2 Ne. 27:9-10; 15-22, JS–Hist. 1:64-65.)

4. The deaf shall hear the words of the book, and the eyes of the blind shall see out of darkness. (29:18)

3rd Event: The Restoration of the Church.

This section includes references to the specific messengers and events of the restoration, as well as to the coming forth of the Church itself. The restoration took place from 1820 to 1836. (See D & C 20; 21:1-10)

1. ? There shall be a root of Jesse, which shall stand for an ensign; to it shall the Gentiles seek. (11:10)

2. Wherefore the Lord said, the people draw near me with their mouth but have removed their heart far from me . . . (29:13; see 2 Ne. 27:25; JS–Hist. 1:19)

3. I will do a marvelous work and a wonder among this people. (29:14; see 2 Ne. 27:26)

4th Event: The Beginning of the Times of the Gentiles.

This event represents the beginning of LDS missionary work, immediately following the restoration of the Church. The present missionary work among the Gentiles is considered as event #7. (See D & C 45:28; JS–Hist. 1:41) (No references in the prophetic section of the Old Testament.)

5th Event: War Poured Out Upon All Nations.

This period began with the U.S. Civil War in 1861 and will continue to the coming of Christ in glory. (See D & C 87:1-8) (No references in the prophetic section of the Old Testament.)

6th Event: The Period of Preparatory Wars.

This event began in conjunction with the U.S. Civil War (5th event). It will continue until the times of the Gentiles are fulfilled (11th event). Early Church leaders explained that during the period of preparatory wars, warfare would tend to overthrow governments which were unfriendly to the L.D.S. missionary effort. New governments would then be formed which would accept our missionary efforts. These wars would thus prepare the way for the spread of the gospel. (See JD 7:186, 188; 18:63-64.) (No references in the prophetic section of the Old Testament.)

7th Event: The Fulness of the Times of the Gentiles.

This period represents the present missionary work of the Church and the first of four periods of missionary labor. It began following the restoration (4th event) and will continue until the Gentiles (primarily the people of Europe and the Americas) reject the Church and persecute its members (10th event). Then the missionaries will be called home and the Gentiles will lose their opportunity to hear the gospel. This will be the fulfilling of the times of the Gentiles (11th event). (See D & C 45:26-33; JS–Hist. 1:41.)

1. He shall bring forth judgment to the Gentiles. (42:1)
2. He will be a light to the Gentiles. (42:6; 49:6)

8th Event: The Rising of Slaves Against Their Masters.

This is being fulfilled as many colonies throughout the world are throwing off the control of their masters. Witness the number of independent states formed since the second world war. Fulfillment can also be seen in the rise of the status of minority groups in the United States. (See D & C 87:4-5; *Conference Report*, October 1958, p. 33.) (No references in the prophetic section of the Old Testament.)

9th Event: The Third World War.

This is a conflict which is expected to take place between the communist forces and the nations of the free world. Reference to it is found primarily in the writings and discourses of certain LDS General Authorities. (See Mosiah Lyman Hancock, *Life Story of Mosiah Lyman Hancock,* p. 29; JI, March 15, 1890, p. 162) (No references in the prophetic section of the Old Testament.)

10th Event: The Saints to Suffer Persecution.

Numerous prophecies by General Authorities have detailed a period of persecution in which the Church and its members will endure great hardships. (See JD 7:185-187; 20:146; *Prophetic Sayings of Heber C. Kimball to Amanda H. Wilcox.*)

11th Event: The Fulfilling of the Times of the Gentiles.

This event will mark the end of concentrated missionary labor among the nations of Europe and the Americas. Events 11, 12, 13, and 14 are expected to take place concurrently. (See JD 18:176-77; 18:64; 8:123.) (No references in the prophetic section of the Old Testament.)

12th Event: The Saints in Foreign Lands Will Gather to the Americas.

Statements and prophecies by early General Authorities foresaw the re-centralization of the Church within the Americas as persecution mounts against it in foreign lands. This is regarded as the time for the call to "come out of Babylon." Events 11, 12, 13, and 14 are expected to take place concurrently. (See D & C 45:69; JS—Matt. 1:27; D & C 115:6; JD 18:64.) (No references in the prophetic section of the Old Testament.)

13th Event: The Gospel Will Be Taken from the Gentiles and Later Given to Israel.

This period is expected to be the era in which the missionary effort will turn from the Gentiles (as their times are fulfilled) and increase in intensity to the house of Israel. The gospel will apparently go first to the Lamanites, then to the Ten Tribes, and then to the scattered house of Judah. Events 11, 12, 13, and 14 are expected to take place concurrently. (See JD 18:177; Mt. 20:16; *Doctrines of Salvation*, III, 258-59.) (No references in the prophetic section of the Old Testament.)

14th Event: God Will Pour Out His Judgments Upon the Earth.

Prophecies pertaining to this period include world-wide destruction from the Lord's desolating scourge, earthquakes, famine and drought, and the sweeping clean of Jackson County, Missouri. These destructions are foreseen as substitutes for the missionary labors among the Gentile nations. Events 11, 12, 13, and 14 are expected to take place concurrently. (See JS 2:45; D & C 88:88-91; JD 8:123; D & C 45:30-33.)

1. Woe to the land shadowing with wings. They shall be cut off and left for the fowls and the beasts to eat. (18:1-6)

15th Event: Internal Wars in the United States.

Internal wars and mobocracy are expected to bring about the collapse of local, state and national governments in the United States. (See HC 3:390-91; 5:394; 6:116; JD 12:344; 8:143.) (No references in the prophetic section of the Old Testament.)

16th Event: World-Wide Revolutions and Deterioration of Governments as the Period of Wars of Total Destruction Begins.

In contrast to the warfare during the period of preparatory wars, the wars during this era will not better the condition of mankind. Instead, it appears that this period will encompass a series of wars and revolutions which will greatly decrease the populations and well-being of the nations of the world. The period of wars of total destruction will continue until the coming of Christ in glory. This period will begin with the internal warfare in the United States (15th event). (See JD 18:341; 21:301.)

17th Event: Saints in America Will Gather to Places of Refuge.

As persecution continues against the Church, and as wars and strife rage in America and throughout the world, it is expected that members of the Church will be summoned to protected areas in order to escape the mobocracy and chaos throughout the land. (See JD 12:345; HC 3:390-91; JD 3:16;4:106.) (No references in the prophetic section of the Old Testament.)

18th Event: The Political Kingdom of God Will Be Established.

A political organization will be established among the Saints in their cities of refuge to govern them. This organization, while secular in its nature, will be comprised mainly of Church members, who will carry out their duties under inspiration. The political kingdom of God will govern the Saints as they return to establish the New Jerusalem and as that center rises to world prominence. (See DEN, Vol. 8, No. 265, Oct. 2, 1875; HC 7:381-82.)

19th Event: The Law of Consecration Will Be Established.

The great distress within the United States and the rapid gathering of the Saints to the cities of refuge will create a need for the renewal of the principles of the United Order and the Law of Consecration. A preliminary introduction of the principle of unity and sharing is expected while the Saints are still in the west. It appears that the principle will not be renewed in its entirety until the Saints return to Jackson County, Missouri. (See DEN 8:265, Oct. 2, 1875; JD 2:57; JD 16:276.)

20th Event: The New Jerusalem and Its Temple Will be Built in Missouri.

A selected group of the Saints will be summoned to journey to Missouri from the West and establish the city of the New Jerusalem in Jackson County. They will be joined during the growth of the city by a huge influx of Indians from North, Central, and South America, by the Ten Tribes who will come from the north, and by increasing numbers of Gentiles who will be drawn to the peace and progress of the city. The city will continue to grow into the millennium. (See DEN 8:265, Oct. 2, 1875; JD 24:156-57; 24:23.)

1. The Lord will lay thy stones with fair colours, and thy foundations with sapphires. (54:12; For interpretive context see 3 Ne. 21; 22)

21st Event: The Conversion of the Lamanites.

In the early days of the New Jerusalem the major period of conversion of the Lamanites, or Indians, is expected to take place. Prophecy depicts these people as gathering to the New Jerusalem area by the millions. They will participate in the building of the city and the temple. (See JD 3:18; 17:301-02; 3 Ne. 21:23-22:3.) (No references in the prophetic section of the Old Testament.)

22nd Event: The Ten Tribes of Israel Will Come From the North to Missouri.

As the New Jerusalem grows, the Ten Tribes of Israel are expected to come from the north to that city. Their coming will somehow be associated with a great earthquake. It is believed that they will stay temporarily in the Missouri area and then move to the land of Israel (31st event). (See *Messenger and Advocate*, Oct. 1835; D & C 133:26-34.)

1. In that time the nation scattered and peeled shall be brought unto Mount Zion. (18:7)

2. The Lord will raise up the tribes of Jacob and restore the preserved of Israel. (49:6)

3. The Lord will also be a light of the Gentiles and the salvation for all the earth. (49 :6)

4. The Lord will cause them to inherit the desolate heritages. (49:8)

5. The Lord will lead his people. He will make all his mountains a way, and his highways shall be exalted. (49:9-11; see D & C 133:26-29)

6. These shall come from far from the north and from the west, and from the land of Sinim (location unknown). (49:12-13)

7. Thy destroyers and they that made thee waste shall go forth of thee. (49:17; see D & C 133:28)

8. The waste and desolate places they inherit will be too crowded. They will object to them and the people there. (49:18-21)

9. The children of the desolate are more than the children of the married wife. (54:1; for interpretive context see 3 Ne. 21; 22)

10. Thy seed shall inherit the desolate cities of the Gentiles. (54:2-3; for interpretive context see 3 Ne. 21; 22)

11. Though the Lord has hidden his face from Israel for a moment, He will remember and comfort His people in that day. (54:4-10; for interpretive context see 3 Ne. 21; 22)

12. A prayer: Return for thy servant's sake, the tribes of thine inheritance. (63:15-19)

23rd Event: Christ Will Come to the New Jerusalem Temple.

A visit of the Savior to the temple in Jackson County is anticipated either shortly before or just after the coming of the Ten Tribes from the north. (See *Millennial Star*, Oct. 22:1845; D & C 97:15-16; 3 Ne. 21:23-25)

1. Thy children shall be taught of the Lord. Thou shalt not fear. (54:13-14; for interpretive context see 3 Ne. 21; 22)

24th Event: 144,000 High Priests Will Be Called.

A group of 144,000 high priests, 12,000 from each of the tribes of Israel, will be called and sent to search out the scattered members of the house of Israel. Their ministry will extend beyond the major period of gathering to the land of Israel (30th and 31st events) and probably beyond the Battle of Armageddon (35th event). (See Rev. 7:1-8; D & C 77:7-11; JD 15:365-66; 16:325-26.)

1. Put on thy strength, O Zion. (52 :1; See D & C 113 :78; also #38)

2. How beautiful upon the mountains are the feet of him that bringeth good tidings by telling Zion thy God reigneth. (52:7; See Mos. 15:13-18)

25th Event: A Period of Great Plagues and Destruction.

As the 144,000 are gathering the scattered people of Israel to their homeland, the earth will undergo a great period of destruction from plagues and warfare. Events 25, 26, 27, and 28 are expected to take place concurrently. (See Rev. 8-11; D & C 29:14-20.)

1. Enemies will gather against them, but not by the Lord. No weapon that is formed against them shall prosper. (54:15-17; For interpretive context see 3 Ne. 21; 22)

26th Event: A Universal Conflict, or Fourth World War, Will Take Place.

Another terrible conflict is to take place, according to prophecy. This war will be the most extensive of the Wars of Total Destruction. Events 25,

26, 27, and 28 are expected to take place concurrently. (See JD 20:150-51; 7:188; 18:339-40; 15:72-73.)

27th Event: The Coming to the Ancient of Days and the Savior to the Council at Adam-ondi-Ahman.

During the universal conflict a huge assembly will convene at Adam-ondi-Ahman, Missouri. Adam (the Ancient of Days) will preside, and will be visited by Christ. Judgment will be held on the nations of the earth, and the kingdom of the earth will be given to the Savior. Events 25, 26, 27, and 28 are expected to take place concurrently. (See HC 3:386-87; 4:207-09; JD 18:338-39; 17:185-86.)

28th Event: The Fall of the Great and Abominable Church.

The great and abominable church is expected to fall, but not become extinct, during the period of universal conflict. It will collapse along with the Christian nations of Europe and the Americas during the universal conflict. Its fall is to take place just before the major period of the gathering of the house of Israel. (See 1 Ne. 14:17 & 22:11-12; 22:13-14; Rev. 17:12-17; 2 Ne. 28:18-20)

29th Event: The Gathering to the New Jerusalem and Its Rise As a World Center of Influence.

The period of world destruction or the universal conflict will serve to diminish the prestige and dominion of many nations. As they decline, the influence of the New Jerusalem will grow. That city will be known for its beauty and righteousness and will gain world prominence as people seek shelter there. (See JD 22:36; 24:31-32.)

30th Event: The Gathering to the Land of Israel of the Scattered Remnants of Judah.

Through the efforts of the 144,000, the scattered members of the house of Judah will be sought out and gathered to their homeland from throughout the world. This will be the second major period of missionary labor. Their gathering will take place before, during, and after the universal conflict, but it is expected to reach its height during the rule of David the Prince. Events 30, 31, and 32 are expected to take place concurrently. The gathering of Judah and the restoration of the Ten Tribes to their homeland are frequent themes in the Old Testament. It is often impossible to determine whether the passage is speaking of just Judah or just Israel, or whether it refers to both. Those passages which seem to refer to both are shown as 30-31 in this listing. References which speak specifically of the gathering of Judah are shown as the 30th event. Specific references to the gathering of the tribes of Israel are shown as the 31st event. (See D & C 45:25; 3 Ne. 20:28-29; 21:28-29.)

1. Loose thyself from the bands of thy neck, O captive daughter of Zion. (52:2; See D & C 113:9-10.)

2. The Lord will redeem the waste places of Jerusalem and all the nations shall see His salvation together. (52:8-10)

30th and 31st Events: General References to the Gathering of the House of Israel.

There are numerous passages which refer to the gathering process but which do not indicate with clarity whether they are speaking of Israel or Judah or both. These have been combined into a special grouping and have been indicated throughout the book as (30-31). This section also includes the passages which specifically establish the return of both Judah and Israel.

1. God will lift up an ensign to the nations from far and will hiss unto them from the end of the earth. (5:26; see 2 Ne. 29:1-2)

2. The light of Israel will be a flame which will devour the land of Assyria in the day that the remnant of Israel (the ten tribes) and those that are escaped of Jacob (the scattered Jews) shall return and shall rely upon the Lord. (10:20-22)

3. Israel and Judah shall be gathered to Palestine. (11:11-12)

4. Lebanon shall be a fruitful field. (29:15-17)

5. The Lord shall be gracious to his people when they dwell in Zion at Jerusalem. He shall make the ground increase. (30:18-24)

6. The desert shall rejoice, and blossom as the rose. (35:1-2)

7. The weak will be strengthened in their journey (to Zion). (35:3-6)

8. Waters and streams will break out in the desert. (35:6-7)

9. A highway shall be there, called the way of holiness, and the ransomed of the Lord shall return to Zion. (35:8-10)

10. Israel will thresh the mountains. God will open up rivers in high places and fountains in the valleys so people will know God has helped Israel. (41:15-20; cf. 30:25-26)

11. The Lord will gather the seed of Israel from the east, west, north, and south. (43:5-7)

12. The Lord will make a way in the wilderness, and rivers in the desert for his chosen people. (43:18-21)

13. He will raise up the tribes of Jacob. (49:6)

14. He will restore the preserved of Israel. (49:6)

15. The Lord will comfort Zion, and make her waste places fertile. (51:3)

16. The Lord will help Israel to return with joy and singing. (51:11-16)

17. Israel will be called out of wickedness and God will protect her in her return. (52:11-12)

18. They shall build the old waste and desolate cities, while strangers tend their flocks. (61:3-5)

19. Cast up the highway, lift up a standard for the people. (62:10)

20. The Lord will send a message throughout the world to Israel that his salvation cometh. (62:11)

21. A seed will inherit the mountains. (65:8-10)

22. Israel travailed and brought forth a man child before her pain came. (66:7-8)

31st Event: The Removal of the Ten Tribes from America to the Land of Israel.

After the Ten Tribes have come from the north to the New Jerusalem and have dwelt in the Americas for a period of time, they are expected to move as a unit to the land of Israel and inherit portions of the land as outlined by Ezekiel. They will join with the house of Judah and form a single, unified government. This section contains prophecies pertaining to their removal from America to Israel and also prophecies which speak of the gathering of Ephraim, the Ten Tribes, or Israel, but do not specify from where they will be gathered. (See JD 18:25; 14:349-50; 20:153; Jer. 31:6-7; 50:19-20; Zech. 10:7-9.)

32nd Event: The Rule of David the Prince.

As the House of Israel returns to their homeland they will combine under the rule of a descendant of the house of David, David the Prince. He will oversee the construction of the temple and will govern during the Battle of Armageddon and on into the millennium. (See HC 6:253; D & C 132:38-39; Hos. 3:5; Is. 4:2; 11:1-5; 55:3-5; Jer. 23:5-6; 30:9; 33:15-26; Ezek. 34:23-24; 37:22-25; 44:1-3; 45:14-25; 46:1-18; Zech. 6:12-13.)

1. In that day (when there will be those of Israel who will have escaped) shall the branch of the Lord be beautiful. (4:2)

2. ? A rod and branch shall come out of the stem of Jesse. (11:1-5)

    A. He shall have the spirit of the Lord. (11:2)

    B. He shall judge the poor and meek with righteousness. (11:3-4)

    C. He shall slay the wicked. (11:4)

3. Prince David will rule. (55:3-5)
    A. He will be a witness to the people.
    B. He will be a leader and commander.
    C. He shall call a nation he does not know.
    D. Nations which do not know him shall run to him.
    E. The Lord will glorify him.

33rd Event: The Construction of the Temple in Jerusalem.

As the house of Israel returns to its homeland in large numbers, it is anticipated that the Jerusalem temple will again be built. Sacrificial worship will also be restored. (See JD 24:215; HC 4:211-12; Amos 9:11; Mic. 4:1-7; Is. 2:1-3; 60:13-17; Ezek. 37:26-27; 40:3-49; 43:13-27; 44:4-31; 45:1-5, 7-13; 47:1-12; Zech. 1:16.)

1. The Lord's house shall be established in the tops of the mountains, and all nations shall flow unto it. (2:1-3)

2. Wood from Lebanon will be brought to adorn the sanctuary. (60:13-17)

34th Event: Israel's Political Affairs.

Rather than being a specific event, this is a general category dealing with the relationships of Israel and other countries in the last days. Most of the prophecies concerning this period are without identifying chronological clues and so cannot be placed in order with exactness. They seem to take place in the period when Israel exists as a nation and before the Battle of Armageddon. It is sometimes difficult to determine whether events should be classed in this category or as a reference to the Battle of Armageddon. (See Amos 9:12; Is. 10:16-19; 11:13-16; 19:14, 16-25; 25:9-12; Zeph. 2:9-10; Obed. 1:18-20; Jer. 48:47; 49:6, 39; Joel 3:19.)

1. The light of Israel will be a flame which will devour the land of Assyria. (10:16-19)

2. Israel and Judah will unite and stand together against their enemies. (11:13-16)

3. The leaders of Egypt are not wise, but make their people err. (19:14)

4. In that day the Lord will heal Egypt and the Egyptians shall know and worship the Lord. (19:16-22)

5. In that day there will be a highway from Egypt to Assyria and Israel will be a blessing in the Lord. (19:23-25)

6. ? The pride of Moab will be brought down. (25:9-12)

35th Event: The Battle of Armageddon.

This great war which is to take place in the land of Israel is one of the most-prophesied-about events of the scriptures. It draws its name from the city of Megiddo in the plain of Esdraelon in north-western Israel. It appears that the surrounding nations, motivated by greed, will attempt to conquer and plunder Israel. The attacking army, Magog, will be led by its general, Gog. As the covenant people are about to succumb to their attack, the Lord will appear on the Mount of Olives. His appearance will rally the people of Israel and they will emerge victorious. Events 35, 36, 37, and 38 are expected to take place concurrently. (See JD 7:188-89; Rev. 11:1-12; D & C 45:48-52; Hos. 1:10-11; 2:14-23; Ezek. 38-39; Zech. 12:8-9; 13:7-9; 14:2; 14:6-15; Joel 1-3.)

1. The Lord will ease himself of his enemies and will purge the dross of Israel. (1:24-25)

2. The Lord will purge Jerusalem. (4:3-4)

3. Israel shall be powerful and lay hold of the prey. (5:27-29)

4. In that day there will be darkness and sorrow in the land. (5:30; see Joel 3:12-15)

5. The Lord shall make a consumption in the midst of all the land. (10:23)

6. ? He shall slay the wicked. (11:4)

7. In that day the Lord will heal Egypt and the Egyptians shall know and worship the Lord. (19:16-22)

8. The Lord has destroyed cities but has aided the poor and the needy. (25:1-5)

9. In that day the Lord will give his people the spirit of judgment and strength in battle. (28:5-6)

10. There shall be water on every high mountain and the light of the sun shall be sevenfold in the day the towers fall and the Lord heals the wound of his people. (30:25-26)

11. The Lord will sift the nations with destruction through devouring fire, scattering, tempest, and hailstones. (30:27-30)

12. At the lifting up of the Lord the nations were scattered. His spoil shall be gathered. (33:2-4)

13. The highways lay waste, the earth mourneth and languisheth. (33:7-8)

14. Those who have warred against Israel shall not be found. (41:11-14)

15. Jerusalem will drink the cup of the Lord's fury. (51:17-18)

16. These two things are come unto thee: Thy sons will lie in the streets of Jerusalem, who have been full of fury of the Lord. (51:19-20; see 2 Ne. 8:19-20; Rev. 11:1-13)

17. The Lord will take His fury from Israel and place it on those who afflict her. (51:22-23)

18. When the enemy shall come in like a flood, the Spirit of the Lord shall lift up a standard against him and the Redeemer shall come to Zion. (59:19-21)

19. The Lord will show His indignation upon His enemies, and the slain of the Lord shall be many. (66:14-17)

20. Men will see the carcasses of those who have transgressed against the Lord. (66:24)

36th Event: The Fall of Rome.

John the Revelator describes the destruction of the great city which sits on seven mountains or hills and is close enough to the sea that the smoke of its destruction can be seen from ships. He shows it as being destroyed at the time of the earthquake during the Battle of Armageddon. Events 35, 36, 37, and 38 are expected to take place concurrently. (See Rev. 16:12-21; 18:1-24.) (No references in the prophetic section of the Old Testament.)

37th Event: The Appearance of Christ on the Mount of Olives.

The Savior will appear on the Mount of Olives as the Battle of Armageddon is raging in Jerusalem and throughout Israel. His appearance will rally the distressed forces of Israel and will enable them to successfully repel their oppressors. He will demonstrate the wounds which have been inflicted upon him to show that he is the crucified Jesus. His appearance will be accompanied by a great earthquake. Events 35, 36, 37, and 38 are expected to take place concurrently. (See Rev. 19:11-16; D & C 45:47-53; *Millennial Star*, 21:583, Sept. 19, 1859; Zech. 13:6; 14:1-21)

1. When the enemy shall come in like a flood, the Spirit of the Lord shall lift up a standard against him and the Redeemer shall come to Zion. (59:19-21; see #35)

2. The Lord shall appear to your joy. There will be noise from the city and the temple as the Lord renders recompense to his enemies. (66:5-6)

38th Event: The Conversion of the House of Israel.

The conversion of the house of Israel is to be culminated with the Savior's appearance on the Mount of Olives. Many of Israel will already have been converted, however, including the Ten Tribes who will have

dwelt in the American Zion, and many who will have been converted by
the 144,000. Events 35, 36, 37, and 38 are expected to take place concurrently. (See D & C 45:51-52; Jer. 31:31-37; Ezek. 39; Zech. 8:8; 12:10;
13:6)

1. He that is left in Jerusalem (after the Lord has purged its filth by judgment and burning) shall be called holy. (4:3)

2. Jacob shall sanctify the name of the Lord and learn doctrine.
(29:22-24)

3. Put on thy strength, O Zion. (52:1; see Moro. 10:31; D & C 113:7-8;
see #24.)

39th Event: Christ Will Come to the Jerusalem Temple and Place His Glory upon Zion.

It is prophesied that the Savior will come to the Jerusalem temple
and will visit with David the prince. This appears to take place after
the Battle of Armageddon, but evidence is not conclusive on this point.
(See Hos. 13:9-10; Is. 60:1-2, 19-20; Ezek. 39:29; Hag. 2:7-9; Zech.
2:10; Joel 3:16-17, 20-21.)

1. The Lord will place his glory (smoke or fire) upon Zion as a defense.
(4:5-6)

2. ? The Lord will place his salvation and glory in Zion. (46:12-13)

3. The glory of the Lord is upon Israel, yet gross darkness covers the
people of the earth. (60:1-2)

4. The glory of the Lord shall be there and provide light. (60:19-20)

5. The Lord will not rest until the righteousness of Jerusalem goes forth
as brightness, and the salvation thereof as a lamp that burneth. (62:1)

40th Event: A Mission to the Heathen Nations.

The Battle of Armageddon will open the way for a third major missionary effort, in which the gospel message will be carried among the heathen nations. This will seemingly be of relatively short duration, and then
will blend into the 4th period of missionary effort, a final mission to all
mankind in preparation for Christ's coming in glory. (See Is. 19:16-25;
61:6-11; Ezek. 37:28; Zech. 2:11.)

1. In that day the Lord will heal Egypt and the Egyptians shall know
and worship the Lord. (19:16-22; #34; see #35)

2. The conversion of Egypt: (19:18-25)

A. Five cities of Egypt shall speak the language of Caanan and shall
swear unto the Lord of Hosts.

B. There shall be an altar to the Lord in Egypt and a pillar to the

Lord at the border.

     C. The Lord shall send Egypt a great savior, and he shall deliver them.

     D. The Egyptians shall know the Lord and shall do sacrifice and vows unto Him.

     E. The Lord shall smite Egypt and then heal it, and they shall return even to the Lord.

     F. There shall be a highway out of Egypt to Assyria, even a blessing in the midst of the land.

     3. Men will call the people of Israel the ministers of God; their seed will be known among the Gentiles. (61:6-9; See #41)

     4. The Lord will cause righteousness and praise to spring forth before all the nations. (61:10-11)

41st Event: Israel's Growth Following the Battle of Armageddon and The Final Mission To All Mankind.

There is to be a final missionary labor conducted throughout the world. It is distinguished from the third period of missionary labor by including the Gentiles (Christian nations) as well as the Heathens (Non-Christian nations). This will be the fourth period of missionary labor. During this period Israel will be increasing in glory and prestige as the world at large reaches the height of its wickedness. This gathering process will be a final call to come out of wickedness. This missionary period will extend into the millennium. References cited in this category deal with the missionary effort and with the rise and glory of Israel following the Battle of Armageddon. It is difficult to distinguish with certainty whether some of the passages deal with pre-millennial or with millennial conditions, since the scriptures give no indication as to what event begins the millennium. (See Mic. 4:1-7; Is. 56:8; 60:3-22; 66:18-19; Zeph. 2:11; 3:9-10; Jer. 3:17; 16:19-20; Ezek. 36:32-36; Zech. 8:20-23; 14:16-21; Mal. 1:11; Joel 2:28-32; 3:18.)

     1. Afterward thou shalt be called the city of righteousness, the faithful city. Zion shall be redeemed with judgment. (1:26-27)

     2. The Lord's house shall be established in the tops of the mountains, and all nations shall flow unto it. (2:1-3; See also 11:6-9; 65:25; #33)

     3. A song of praise unto God when his goodness is known throughout all the earth. (12:1-6)

     4. We have a strong city where only the righteous may enter. (26:1-4)

     5. The Lord has made the nation increase. (26:12-18; see #40)

6. Thou art glorified: thou hadst removed the nation far unto all the ends of the earth. We have not wrought any deliverance in the earth, neither have the inhabitants of the world fallen. (26:15-18)

7. The Lord is exalted and has filled Zion with judgment and righteousness. (33:4-6)

8. The Lord which gathereth the outcasts of Israel will gather others to him, beside those that are gathered unto him. (56:8)

9. The Gentiles and kings shall come to thy light. (60:3-4)

10. The abundance of the sea shall be given to Israel; the surrounding nations will bring their treasures. (60:5-7)

11. The sons of strangers shall build up thy walls, and their kings shall minister unto thee. (60:10-11)

12. The nation and kingdom that will not serve thee shall perish. (60:12)

13. Those that despised Israel and the sons of those that afflicted her will bow down to her. (60:14)

14. Thou shalt suck the milk of the Gentiles and kings. (60:16)

15. Violence shall no more be heard in the land. (60:18)

16. A little one shall become a thousand, and a small one a strong nation. (60:21-22)

17. The Lord will cause righteousness and praise to spring forth before all the nations. (61:10-11; see #40)

18. The good things of Palestine will no longer be given to enemies. (62:8-9)

19. They shall call them the Holy People, the redeemed of the Lord. (62:12)

20. Jerusalem shall be comforted. She shall have peace like a river and the glory of the Gentiles like a flowing stream. (66:9-13)

21. The nations will gather to Jerusalem to see the Lord's glory. Those that have escaped will be sent to the nations to declare the glory of God among the Gentiles. (66:18-19)

22. The nations will help bring the remaining members of Israel as an offering to the Lord. (66:19-21)

23. Israel's seed and all flesh will come up to worship him. (66:22-23)

42nd Event: Christ's Coming in Glory.

Christ will come in glory, accompanied by the hosts of heaven. His coming will be visible to all mankind. The righteous living will be caught up to descend with Him and the righteous dead will come forth from their graves. The earth will be burned and the wicked will be destroyed at His coming. (See *Millennial Star*, 21:583, Sept. 10, 1859; D & C 88:95-110; 29:9-13; 133:46-52; 133:21-25; 101:24-25; Is. 24:19-20; 34:1-15; 40:5-8; 63:1-6; Nah. 1:2-7; Mal. 3:5-6; 4:1.)

1. The destruction of the transgressors and of the sinners shall be together; they shall be burned and consumed. (1:28-31)

2. Fear and a terrible earthquake will come when Christ is exalted. (2:10-21)

3. The day of the Lord is at hand. (13:6-13)

A. Men shall be afraid.

B. The day of the Lord is cruel both with wrath and with fierce anger.

C. The sun, moon, and stars shall not give their light.

D. The Lord will punish the world.

E. A man will be more precious than fine gold.

F. The Lord will shake the heavens, and the earth shall remove out of her place.

4. The earth is desolate, with few men left. (24:1-12)

5. The earth is cleansed because the people have transgressed the laws, changed the ordinances, and broken the everlasting covenant. (24:5-6)

6. The fires of that day will cause the righteous to sing praises to the Lord. (24:13-15)

7. The earth, in this day shall (24:19-20)

A. Be utterly broken down.

B. Be clean dissolved.

C. Be moved exceedingly.

D. Reel to and fro like a drunkard.

E. Be removed like a cottage.

F. Fall and not rise again.

8. The wicked shall be cast into the (spirit) prison, and shall not be visited for many days. (24:21-22)

9. He will rend the veil and reveal himself to the people. (25:7; see D & C 67:10; 38:8)

10. The Lord will destroy the wicked because they will not learn righteousness. (26:5-11)

11. The Lord will come to punish the inhabitants of the earth for their iniquity. (26:20-21)

12. The terrible one is brought to naught, and the scorner is consumed, and all that watch for iniquity are cut off. (29:19-21)

13. The treacherous spoiler will be spoiled. (33:1)

14. The Lord is exalted, the wicked are burned with fire. (33:10-13)

15. The Lord has destroyed the armies of all nations. Their dead stink. (34:1-3)

16. The host of heaven shall be dissolved, and the heavens shall be rolled together as a scroll. (34:4)

17. The land shall be turned into unquenchable burning, for it is the day of the Lord's vengeance. (34:5-10)

18. The nobles will be removed and thorns will come up in the palace. (34:11-15)

19. Every valley shall be exalted, and every mountain and hill shall be made low. (40:3-4)

20. The glory of the Lord shall be revealed, and all flesh shall see it together. (40:5)

21. Temporal things shall wither but the word of God shall stand forever. (40:6-8)

22. The wicked shall be destroyed, but the Lord's righteousness shall be forever. (51:6-8)

23. The Lord will come in His glory, dressed in red apparel, and tread down the wicked. (63:1-6; See D & C 133:46-52)

24. A prayer that the Lord will cleanse the earth with fire. (64:1-3)

43rd Event: The First Resurrection, or Resurrection of the Righteous.

Many of the righteous dead will be resurrected at the time of Christ's coming in glory. Some of the dead may also be resurrected long before his advent. (See D & C 88:95-110; 128:22; JD 25:33-34; 9:27; Hos. 13:14; Zech. 9:11-12; Mal. 3:16-18.)

1. He will swallow up death in victory. (25:8)

44th Event: The Millennium.

The millennium is to be a thousand years of peace and prosperity during which the Savior will rule here upon the earth. The scriptures do not clearly define what event will begin the millennial era, but it is generally regarded as beginning with Christ's coming in glory. (See D & C 63:50-52; Rev. 20:1-3; D & C 101:32-34; Mic. 4:3-4; Obad. 1:21; Zech. 3:10; 9:10.)

1. Out of Zion shall go forth the law, and the word of the Lord from Jerusalem. (2:3)

2. Nation shall not lift up the sword against nation. (2:4)

3. Of the increase of his government and peace there shall be no end, upon the throne of David, and upon his kingdom, to order it, and to establish it with judgment, and with justice from henceforth even for ever. (9:7)

4. Peace during the millennium. (11:6-9)

5. ? In that day there shall be a root of Jesse, which shall stand for an ensign; to it shall the Gentiles seek. (11:10)

6. The Lord shall reign in mount Zion, and in Jerusalem. (24:23)

7. He will give the people a feast of fat things (rich blessings). (25:6)

8. A king shall reign in righteousness, and princes shall rule in judgment. (32:1-4)

9. No longer will the vile person be honored as good, nor be allowed to destroy the poor with lying words. (32:5-8)

10. The spirit shall be poured out from on high and the righteous will dwell in quietness and assurance for ever. (32:15-20)

11. The Lord God will rule from Jerusalem. (40:9-11)

12. He shall set judgment in the earth unto truth. (42:3-4)

13. The Lord will punish the wicked among the people of Israel. (65:11-16)

14. A child shall live to one hundred. (65:18-20)

15. They shall build and enjoy the work of their hands. (65:21-24)

16. They shall not hurt or destroy; there shall be peace. (65:25)

17. The Lord will create a new heaven and a new earth. (66:22)

45th Event: The Battle of Gog and Magog.

At the end of the millennial era wickedness will again break out and Satan will be loosed. A struggle will take place between the forces of good and the hosts of evil. The evil forces are personified as Gog and Magog. They are expected to encompass the saints in the "beloved city" and then be destroyed by fire from heaven. (See Rev. 20:7-10; HC 5:298; JD 16:119-20, 322; D & C 88:111-116; 43:31-33)

1. The wicked shall be destroyed, but the Lord's righteousness will be forever. (51:7-8; see #42, #48)

46th Event: The Second Resurrection, or Resurrection of the Unrighteous.

A second resurrection will take place in which the remainder of the dead will regain their bodies. These are the people who will inherit the telestial kingdom or will become sons of perdition. (See D & C 76:81-85; 88:100-102; 29:26-30; Rev. 20:13)

1. He will bring prisoners from the (spirit?) prison. (42:7)

2. He shall release prisoners. (49:9)

47th Event: The Final Judgment.

A final judgment will be held in which all mankind will come before the Savior to be judged for their works. (See D & C 19:1-3; 38:5; Rev. 20:12-15; Mos. 27:31; 2 Ne. 9:13-16; JD 17:182.)

1. The Lord has sworn that every knee shall bow and every tongue shall acknowledge Him. (45:23-25)

48th Event: The Crowning and Exalting of Christ and the Saints.

At the end of the judgment Christ will present the kingdom of the earth to the Father and in turn be crowned with power and glory. (See D & C 76:106-108; 1 Cor. 15:22-26, 28; D & C 130:9; D & C 76:54-62)

1. The righteous shall dwell (with God) in everlasting burnings. (33:14-17)

2. Jerusalem shall be a quiet habitation with a tabernacle. It shall not be removed. (33:18-24)

3. The heavens shall vanish and the earth shall wax old like a garment, but the Lord's salvation will continue forever. (51:4-6; see #49)

4. The wicked shall be destroyed, but the Lord's righteousness shall be forever. (51:7-8; see #42; #45)

49th Event: The Dissolution of the Earth and Its Heaven.

After the final judgment and the crowning of the Savior, the earth is to return to its elemental state and pass away into space. The cities of the old and New Jerusalem and their occupants will be caught up into the air until the earth is restored. (See D & C 88:25-26; JD 1:331; 18:346-47.)

1. The heavens shall vanish and the earth shall wax old like a garment, but the Lord's salvation will continue forever. (51:6; see #48)

50th Event: The Re-creation of the Earth as a Celestial World.

The earth is to be re-created as a celestialized sphere. The old and the New Jerusalem will descend upon it and will also become sanctified and immortal. (See Rev. 21:1-27; JD 18:322; D & C 88:17-20; 29:23-25)

Summary

1. Prophecies concerning the last days are the largest single doctrinal theme found in the scriptures.

2. The Old Testament prophets discussed or alluded to thirty-seven of a selected group of fifty important happenings which are prophesied to take place in the last days. They prophesied extensively concerning fourteen events in particular:

A. the restoration of the Church,

B. the coming of the ten tribes from the north to Missouri,

C. a universal conflict, or fourth world war,

D. the gathering of Judah to the land of Israel,

E. the removal of the ten tribes from America to the land of Israel,

F the rule of David the Prince,

G. the construction of the temple in Jerusalem,

H. Israel's political affairs in the last days,

I. the Battle of Armageddon,

J. the conversion of Judah and Israel to Christ,

K. Christ's rule as king in Israel,

L. missionary work to the heathens and gentiles following the Battle of Armageddon,

M. Christ's coming in glory, and

N. the millennium.

3. Of these 14 items, the prophet Isaiah made significant prophecies concerning eleven of them.

4. The purpose of scriptural study is to understand doctrine and to apply it for the betterment of one's life.

The wolf also shall dwell with the lamb, and the leopard shall lie down with the kid; and the calf and the young lion and the fatling together; and a little child shall lead them.

And the cow and the bear shall feed; their young ones shall lie down together: and the lion shall eat straw like the ox.

And the sucking child shall play on the hole of the asp, and the weaned child shall put his hand on the cockatrice' den.

They shall not hurt nor destroy in all my holy mountain: for the earth shall be full of the knowledge of the LORD, as the waters cover the sea.

(Isaiah 11:6-9)

Part IV

INSIGHTS FROM THE INSPIRED VERSION

For the LORD shall comfort Zion: he will comfort all her waste places; and he will make her wilderness like Eden, and her desert like the garden of the LORD; joy and gladness shall be found therein, thanksgiving, and the voice of melody.

(Isaiah 51:3)

How beautiful upon the mountains are the feet of him that bringeth good tidings, that publisheth peace; that bringeth good tidings of good, that publisheth salvation; that saith unto Zion, Thy God reigneth!

Thy watchmen shall lift up the voice; with the voice together shall they sing: for they shall see eye to eye, when the LORD shall bring again Zion.

Break forth into joy, sing together, ye waste places of Jerusalem: for the LORD hath comforted his people, he hath redeemed Jerusalem.

The LORD hath made bare his holy arm in the eyes of all the nations; and all the ends of the earth shall see the salvation of our God.

(Isaiah 52:7-10)

15

INSIGHTS FROM THE INSPIRED VERSION

King James Translation

2:2—And it shall come to pass in the last days, that the mountain of the Lord's house . . .

2:5—O house of Jacob, come ye, and let us walk in the light of the Lord.

2:6—Therefore thou hast forsaken thy people the house of Jacob, because they be replenished from the east and are soothsayers like the Philistines . . .

2:9—And the mean man boweth down, and the great man humbleth himself: therefore forgive them not.

Inspired Version

2:2—And it shall come to pass in the last days, **when** the mountain of the Lord's house . . .

2:5—O house of Jacob, come ye, and let us walk in the light of the Lord; **yea, come, for ye have all gone astray, every one to his wicked ways**.

2:6—Therefore, O Lord, thou hast forsaken thy people the house of Jacob, because they be replenished from the east, and **hearken unto the soothsayers** like the Philistines . . .

2:9—And the mean man boweth **not** down, and the great man humbleth himself **not**; therefore forgive them not.

King James Translation

2:10—Enter into the rock, and hide thee in the dust, for fear of the Lord, and for the glory of his majesty.

2:11—The lofty looks of man shall be humbled, and the haughtiness of men shall be bowed down . . .

2:12—For the day of the Lord of hosts shall be upon every one that is proud and lofty, and upon every one that is lifted up; and he shall be brought low:

2:13—And upon all the cedars of Lebanon, that are high and lifted up, and upon all the oaks of Bashan.

2:14—And upon all the high mountains, and upon all the hills that are lifted up,

2:15—And upon every high tower, and upon every fenced wall,

2:16—And upon all the ships of Tarshish, and upon all pleasant pictures.

2:19— . . . for fear of the Lord

2:20— . . . and his idols of gold, which they made each one for himself to worship,

2:21— . . . for fear of the Lord, and for the glory of his majesty, when

Inspired Version

2:10—**O ye wicked ones**, enter into the rock, and hide **ye** in the dust; for the fear of the Lord and **his majesty shall smite thee**.

2:11—**And it shall come to pass that** the lofty looks of man shall be humbled, and the hautiness of **man** shall be bowed down . . .

2:12—For the day of the Lord of hosts **soon cometh upon all nations; yea, upon every one; yea**, upon the proud and lofty, and upon every one **who** is lifted up, and he shall be brought low.

2:13—**Yea, and the day of the Lord shall come** upon all the cedars of Lebanon, **for they are** high and lifted up; and upon all the oaks of Bashan.

2:14—And upon all the high mountains, and upon all the hills, **and upon all the nations** which are lifted up;

2:15—**And upon every people**, and upon every high tower, and upon every fenced wall,

2:16—**And upon all the ships of the sea**, and upon all the ships of Tarshish, and upon all pleasant pictures.

2:19— . . . for **the** fear of the Lord . . .

2:20— . . . and his idols of gold which **he hath made** for himself to worship, . . .

2:21— . . . for **the** fear of the Lord **shall come upon them, and the**

King James Translation

he ariseth to shake terribly the earth.

3:1— . . . the stay and the staff, the whole stay of bread and the whole stay of water,

3:4—And I will give children to be their princes, and babes shall rule over them.

3:6— . . . saying, Thou hast clothing, be thou our ruler, and let this ruin be under thy hand:

3:8— . . . their tongue and their doings are against the Lord, to provoke the eyes of his glory.

3:9—The shew of their countenance doth witness against them; and they declare their sin as Sodom, they hide it not. Woe unto their souls!
3:10—Say ye to the righteous that it shall be well with him:
3:11—Woe unto the wicked! it shall be ill with him: for the reward of his hands shall be given him.
3:12—. . . they which lead thee . . .

3:14— . . . the spoil of the poor is in your houses.
3:15—What mean ye that ye beat my people to pieces, and grind the faces of the poor? saith the Lord God of hosts.

Inspired Version

majesty of the Lord shall smite them, when he ariseth to shake terribly the earth.

3:1— . . . The stay and the staff, the whole **staff** of bread, and the whole stay of water,

3:4—And I will give children **unto them** to be their princes, and babes shall rule over them.

3:6— . . . **and shall say,** Thou hast clothing, be thou our ruler, and let **not** this ruin come under thy hand;

3:8— . . . their tongues and their doings **have been** against the Lord, to provoke the eyes of his glory.
3:9—The **show** of their countenance doth witness against them; and **doth declare their sin to be** even as Sodom, they cannot hide it. Woe unto their souls!
3:10—Say **unto** the righteous, that it is well with **them**; . . .
3:11—Woe unto the wicked! **for they shall perish**; for the reward of **their** hands shall be **upon them**.
3:12— . . . they **who** lead thee

3:14— . . . **and** the spoil of the poor is in your houses.
3:15—What mean ye? **ye** beat my people to pieces, and grind the faces of the poor, saith the Lord God of hosts.

King James Translation

3:18—In that day the Lord will take away the bravery of their tinkling ornaments about their feet, and their cauls, and their round tires like the moon,

3:26— . . . and she being desolate shall sit upon the ground.

4:1—And in that day seven women shall take hold of one man . . .

4:3—And it shall come to pass that he that is left in Zion, and he that remaineth in Jerusalem . . .

4:5— . . . for upon all the glory shall be a defense.

5:1—Now will I sing . . .

5:5— . . . and break down the wall . . .

5:9—. . . many houses shall be desolate, even great and fair, without inhabitant.

5:11— . . . that they may follow strong drink; that continue until night, till wine inflame them!

6:9— . . . Hear ye indeed, but understand not; and see ye indeed, but perceive not.

6:12— . . . and there be a great forsaking in the midst of the land.

6:13— But yet in it shall be a tenth, and it shall return, and shall be eaten:

8:19— . . . should not a people seek unto their God? for the living to the dead?

Inspired Version

3:18—In that day the Lord will take away the bravery of tinkling ornaments, and cauls, and round tires like the moon.

3:26— . . . and she **shall be** desolate **and** shall sit upon the ground.

3:27—(The wording is identical with 4:1 in the King James Translation. The verse is made a part of Chapter 3.)

4:2—And it shall come to pass, **they** that are left in Zion, and he that remaineth in Jerusalem . . .

4:4— . . . for upon all the glory **of Zion** shall be a defense.

5:1—**And then** will I sing . . .

5:5— . . . and **I will break** down the wall . . .

5:9— . . . many houses shall be desolate, and great and fair **cities** without inhabitant.

5:11— . . . that they may follow strong drink, **and** that continue until night, **and** wine inflame them!

6:9— . . . Hear ye indeed, but **they understood** not; and see ye indeed, but **they perceived** not.

6:12— . . . **for** there **shall** be a great forsaking in the midst of the land.

6:13— But yet in it there shall be a tenth, and **they** shall return, and shall be eaten;

8:19—. . . should not a people seek unto their God? for the living to **hear from** the dead?

King James Translation

9:1— . . . by the way of the sea . . .

9:3—Thou hast multiplied the nation, and not increased the joy:

9:7— Of the increase of his government and peace there shall be no end . . .

9:17— . . . for every one is an hypocrite . . .

10:7— . . . but it is in his heart to destroy and cut off nations not a few.

10:10—As my hand hath found the kingdoms . . .

10:13—For he saith, By the strength of my hand I have done it, and by my wisdom; for I am prudent: and I have removed the bounds of the people . . .

13:2— Lift ye up a banner . . .

13:3—. . . I have also called my mighty ones for mine anger, even them that rejoice in my highness.

13:15—Every one that is found shall be thrust through; and every one that is joined unto them shall fall by the sword.

13:22— . . . and her days shall not be prolonged.

Inspired Version

9:1— . . . by the way of the **Red** sea . . .

9:3— . . . Thou hast multiplied the nation, and increased the joy;

9:7— Of the increase of his government and peace there **is** no end . . .

9:17— . . . for every one **of them** is a hypocrite . . .

10:7— . . . but in his heart **it is** to destroy and cut off nations not a few.

10:10—As my hand hath **founded** the kingdoms . . .

10:13—For he saith, By the strength of my hand, **and by my** wisdom I have done **these things**; for I am prudent, and I have **moved** the **borders** of the people . . .

13:2—Lift ye up **my** banner

13:3— . . . I have also called my mighty ones, for mine anger is **not upon** them that rejoice in my highness.

13:15—Every one that is **proud** shall be thrust through; and every one that is joined **to the wicked** shall fall by the sword.

13:22— . . . and her days shall not be prolonged; **for I will destroy her speedily; yea, for I will be merciful unto my people, but the wicked shall perish.**

King James Translation

14:2—And the people shall take them, and bring them to their place: and the house of Israel shall possess them . . .

14:3— And it shall come to pass in the day that the Lord shall give thee rest from thy sorrow, and from thy fear, and from the hard bondage wherein thou was made to serve,

14:4—That thou shalt take up this proverb against the king of Babylon, and say, How hath the oppressor ceased! the golden city ceased!

14:16—They that see thee shall narrowly look upon thee, and consider thee, saying, Is this the man . . .

14:19— . . . and as the raiment of those that are slain, . . .

16:6—We have heard of the pride of Moab; he is very proud: even of his haughtiness, and his pride, and his wrath: but his lies shall not be so.

23:10— . . . there is no more strength.

29:2—Yet will I distress Ariel and there shall be heaviness and sorrows; and it shall be unto me as Ariel.

Inspired Version

14:2—And the people shall take them, and bring them to their place: **yea, from far, unto the end of the earth, and they shall return to their land of promise**, and the house of Israel shall possess them . . .

14:3—And it shall come to pass in **that** day that the Lord shall give thee rest from thy sorrow and from thy fear, and from the hard bondage wherein thou was made to serve.

14:4—**And it shall come to pass in that day** that thou shalt take up this proverb against the king of Babylon, and say, How hath the oppressor ceased! the golden city ceased!

14:16—They that see thee shall narrowly look upon thee, and **shall** consider thee, **and shall say**, Is this the man . . .

14:19— . . . and the **remnant** of those that are slain, . . .

16:6—We have heard of the pride of Moab; of his haughtiness and his pride, for he is very proud; and his wrath, his lies, **and all his evil works**.

23:10— . . . there is no more strength **in thee**.

29:2—Yet I will distress Ariel, and there shall be heaviness and sorrow; **for thus hath the Lord said unto me, It shall be unto Ariel**:

King James Translation

29:3—And I will camp against thee round about, and will lay siege against thee with a mount, and I will raise forts against thee.

29:4—And thou shalt be brought down and shalt speak out of the ground, and thy speech shall be low out of the dust, and thy voice shall be, as one that hath a familiar spirit, out of the ground, and thy speech shall whisper out of the dust.

29:5—Moreover the multitude of thy strangers . . .

29:6—Thou shalt be visited of the Lord of hosts . . .

29:8—It shall even be as when an hungry man dreameth, and, behold, he eateth; but he awaketh, and his soul is empty; or as when a thirsty man dreameth, and, behold, he drinketh; but he awaketh, and, behold he is faint, and his soul hath appetite: so shall the multitude of all the nations be, that fight against mount Zion.

29:9—Stay yourselves, and wonder; cry ye out, and cry: they are drunken, but not with wine; they stagger, but not with strong drink.

29:10—For the Lord hath poured out upon you the spirit of deep sleep, and hath closed your eyes:

Inspired Version

29:3—**That I the Lord** will camp against **her** round about, and will lay siege against **her** with a mount, and I will raise forts against **her**.

29:4—And **she** shall be brought down, and shall speak out of the ground, and **her** speech shall be low out of the dust; and **her** voice shall be as **of** one that hath a familiar spirit, out of the ground, and **her** speech shall whisper out of the dust.

29:5—Moreover the multitude of **her** strangers . . .

29:6—**For they** shall be visited of the Lord of hosts . . .

29:8—**Yea, it shall be unto them even as unto** a hungry man who dreameth, and behold, he eateth, but he awaketh and his soul is empty; **or like unto** a thirsty man who dreameth, and behold, he drinketh, but he awaketh, and behold, he is faint, and his soul hath appetite. **Yea, even** so shall the multitude of all the nations be, that fight against mount Zion.

29:9—**For, behold, all ye that do iniquity**, stay yourselves, and wonder; **for ye shall** cry out, and cry: yea, **ye shall be** drunken, but not with wine; ye shall stagger, but not with strong drink.

29:10—For, **behold**, the Lord hath poured out upon you the spirit of deep sleep. **For, behold, ye** have closed your eyes, and **ye have**

King James Translation

the prophets and your rulers, the seers hath he covered.

Inspired Version

rejected the prophets, and your rulers; and the seers hath he covered because of your iniquities.

29:11—And it shall come to pass that the Lord God shall bring forth unto you the words of a book; and they shall be the words of them which have slumbered.

29:12—And behold, the book shall be sealed; and in the book shall be a revelation from God, from the beginning of the world to the ending thereof.

29:13—Wherefore because of the things which are sealed up, the things which are sealed shall not be delivered in the day of the wickedness and abominations of the people. Wherefore, the book shall be kept from them.

29:14—But the book shall be delivered unto a man, and he shall deliver the words of the book, which are the words of those who haves slumbered in the dust; and he shall deliver these words to another, but the words that are sealed he shall not deliver, neither shall he deliver the book.

29:15—For the book shall be sealed by the power of God, and the revelation which was sealed shall be kept in the book until the own due time of the Lord, that they come forth; for, behold, they reveal all things from the foundation of the world unto the end thereof.

King James Translation

Inspired Version

29:16—And the day cometh, that the words of the book which were sealed shall be read upon the housetops; and they shall be read by the power of Christ; and all things shall be revealed unto the children of men which ever have been among the children of men, and which ever will be, even unto the end of the earth.

29:17—Wherefore, at that day when the book shall be delivered unto the man of whom I have spoken, the book shall be hid from the eyes of the world, that the eyes of none shall behold it, save it be that three witnesses shall behold it by the power of God, besides him to whom the book shall be delivered; and they shall testify to the truth of the book and the things therein.

29:18—And there is none other which shall view it, save it be a few according to the will of God, to bear testimony of his word unto the children of men; for the Lord God hath said, that the words of the faithful should speak as it were from the dead.

29:19—Wherefore, the Lord God will proceed to bring forth the words of the book; and in the mouth of as many witnesses as seemeth him good will he establish his word; and woe be unto him that rejecteth the word of God.

King James Translation

29:11—And the vision of all is become unto you as the words of a book that is sealed, which men deliver to one that is learned, saying, Read this, I pray thee: and he saith, 1 cannot; for it is sealed.

29:12—And the book is delivered to him that is not learned, saying, Read this, I pray thee: and he saith, I am not learned.

Inspired Version

29:20—But, behold, it shall come to pass that the Lord God shall say unto him to whom he shall deliver the book, Take these words which are not sealed and deliver them to another, that he may show them unto the learned, saying, Read this I pray thee.

29:21—And the learned shall say, Bring hither the book and I will read them; and now because of the glory of the world, and to get gain will they say this, and not for the glory of God. And the man shall say, I cannot bring the book for it is sealed. Then shall the learned say, I cannot read it.

29:22—Wherefore it shall come to pass, that the Lord will deliver again the book and the words thereof to him that is not learned; and the man that is not learned shall say I am not learned. Then shall the Lord God say unto him, The learned shall not read them, for they have rejected them, and I am able to do mine own work; wherefore thou shalt read the words which I shall give unto thee.

29:23—Touch not the things which are sealed, for I will bring them forth in mine own due time; for I will show unto the children of men that I am able to do mine own work.

29:24—Wherefore, when thou hast read the words which I have

King James Translation

Inspired Version

commanded thee, and obtained the witnesses which I have promised unto thee, then shalt thou seal up the book again, and hide it up unto me, that I may preserve the words which thou hast not read until I see fit in mine own wisdom to reveal all things unto the children of men. 29:25—For behold, I am God; and I am a God of miracles; and I will show unto the world that I am the same, yesterday, to-day, and for ever; and I work not among the children of men, save it be according to their faith.

29:26—And again it shall come to pass, that the Lord shall say unto him that shall read the words that shall be delivered him, Forasmuch as this people draw near unto me with their mouth, and with their lips do honor me, but have removed their hearts far from me, and their fear toward me is taught by the precepts of men, therefore I will proceed to do a marvelous work among this people: yea, a marvelous work and a wonder; for the wisdom of their wise and learned shall perish, and the understanding of their prudent shall be hid.

29:27—And woe unto them that seek deep to hide their counsel from the Lord. And their works are in the dark; and they say, Who seeth us and who knoweth us?

29:13—Wherefore the Lord said, Forasmuch as this people draw near me with their mouth, and with their lips do honour me, but have removed their hearts far from me, and their fear toward me is taught by the precept of men:
29:14—Therefore, behold, I will proceed to do a marvellous work among this people, even a marvellous work and a wonder: for the wisdom of their wise men shall perish, and the understanding of their prudent men shall be hid.
29:15—Woe unto them that seek deep to hide their counsel from the Lord, and their works are in the dark, and they say, Who seeth us? and who knoweth us?

King James Translation

29:16—Surely your turning of things upside down shall be esteemed as the potter's clay: for shall the work say of him that made it, He made me not? or shall the thing framed say of him that framed it, He had no understanding?

29:17—It is not yet a very little while, and Lebanon shall be turned into a fruitful field, and the fruitful field shall be esteemed as a forest.

29:18—And in that day shall the deaf hear the words of the book, and the eyes of the blind shall see out of obscurity, and out of darkness.

29:19—The meek also shall increase their joy in the Lord, and the poor among men shall rejoice in the Holy One of Israel.

29:20—For the terrible one is brought to naught, and the scorner is consumed, and all that watch for iniquity are cut off:

29:21—That make a man an offender for a word, and lay a snare for him that reproveth in the gate, and turn aside the just for a thing of naught.

Inspired Version

And they also say, Surely your turning of things upside down shall be esteemed as the potter's clay.

29:28—But behold, I will show unto them, saith the Lord of hosts, that I know all their works. For, shall the work say of him that made it, He made me not? or shall the thing framed say of him that framed it, He had no understanding?

29:29—But behold, saith the Lord of hosts, I will show unto the children of men, that it is not yet a very little while, and Lebanon shall be turned into a fruitful field; and the fruitful field shall be esteemed as a forest.

29:30—And in that day shall the deaf hear the words of the book; and the eyes of the blind shall see out of obscurity and out of darkness;

and the meek also shall increase, and their joy shall be in the Lord; and the poor among men shall rejoice in the Holy One of Israel.

29:31—For, assuredly as the Lord liveth, they shall see that the terrible one is brought to naught, and the scorner is consumed, and all that watch for iniquity are cut off, and they that make a man an offender for a word, and lay a snare for him that reproveth in the gate, and turn aside the just for a thing of naught.

King James Translation

29:22—Therefore thus saith the Lord, who redeemed Abraham, concerning the house of Jacob, Jacob shall not now be ashamed, neither shall his face now wax pale.

29:23—But when he seeth his children, the work of mine hands, in the midst of him, they shall sanctify my name, and sanctify the Holy One of Jacob, and shall fear the God of Israel.

29:24—They also that erred in spirit shall come to understanding, and they that murmured shall learn doctrine.

32: 14—Because the palaces shall be forsaken; the multitude of the city shall be left; . . .

34:7—And the unicorns shall come down with them, . . .

34:16—Seek ye out of the book of the Lord, and read: no one of these shall fail, none shall want her mate: for my mouth it hath commanded, and his spirit it hath gathered them.

34:17—he hath cast the lot for them, and his hand hath divided it unto them by line: . . .

35:8—And an highway shall be there, and a way, and it shall be called The way of holiness; the

Inspired Version

29:32—Therefore, thus saith the Lord who redeemed Abraham concerning the house of Jacob, Jacob shall not now be ashamed, neither shall his face now wax pale; but

when he seeth his children, the work of my hands, in the midst of him, they shall sanctify my name, and sanctify the Holy One of Jacob, and shall fear the God of Israel. They also that erred in spirit shall come to understanding, and they that murmured shall learn doctrine.

32:14—Because the palaces shall be forsaken; the **houses** of the city shall be left **desolate**; . . .

34:7—And the **reem** shall come down with them, . . .

34:16—Seek ye out of the book of the Lord, and read **the names written therein**; No one of these shall fail; none shall want **their** mate; for my mouth it hath commanded, and **my** spirit it hath gathered them.

34:17—And **I** have cast the lot for them, and **I** have divided it unto them by line; . . .

35:8—And a highway shall be there; **for a way shall be cast up**, and it shall be called the way of

King James Translation

unclean shall not pass over it; but it shall be for those: the wayfaring men, though fools, shall not err therein.

36:5—I say, sayest thou, (but they are but vain words) I have counsel and strength for war: . . .

37:17— . . . and hear all the words of Sennacherib, which hath sent to reproach the living God.

37:32—For out of Jerusalem shall go forth a remnant, and they that escape out of mount Zion: the zeal of the Lord of hosts shall do this.

37:36—Then the angel of the Lord went forth, and smote in the camp of the Assyrians a hundred and fourscore and five thousand: and when they arose early in the morning, behold, they were all dead corpses.

38:15— . . . he hath both spoken unto me, and himself hath done it: I shall go softly all my years in the bitterness of my soul.

38:16—O Lord, by these things men live, and in all these things is the life of my spirit: so wilt thou recover me, and make me to live.

Inspired Version

holiness. The unclean shall not pass over **upon** it; but it shall be **cast up** for those **who are clean**, and the wayfaring men, though **they are accounted** fools, shall not err therein.

36:5—I say, thy words are but vain when thou sayest, I have counsel and strength for war. . . .

37:17— . . . and hear all the words of Sennacherib, which **he** hath sent to reproach the living God.

37:32—for out of Jerusalem shall go forth a remnant; and they that escape out of **Jerusalem shall come up upon mount Zion**; the zeal of the Lord of hosts shall do this.

37:36—Then the angel of the Lord went forth, and smote in the camp of the Assyrians a hundred and four-score and five thousand, and when they **who were left** arose, early in the morning, behold they were all dead corpses.

38:15— . . . he hath both spoken unto me, and himself hath **healed me**. I shall go softly all my years, **that I may not walk** in the bitterness of my soul.

38:16—Oh Lord, **thou who art the life of my spirit, in whom I live**; so wilt thou recover me, and make me to live; **and in all these things will I praise thee.**

King James Translation

38:17—Behold, for peace had great bitterness: but thou hast in love to my soul delivered it from the pit of corruption: . . .

41:28—For I beheld, and there was no man; even among them, . . .

42:19—Who is blind, but my servant? or deaf, as my messenger that I sent? who is blind as he that is perfect, and blind as the Lord's servant?
42:20—Seeing many things, but thou observest not; opening the ears, but he heareth not.

42:21—The Lord is well pleased for his righteousness' sake; he will magnify the law, and make it honorable.

42:22—But this is a people robbed and spoiled; they are all of them snared in holes, and they are hid in prison houses: they are for a prey, and none delivereth; for a spoil, and none saith, Restore.

42:23—Who among you will give ear to this? who will hearken and hear for the time to come?

Inspired Version

38:17—Behold, **I had great bitterness instead of peace**, but thou hast in love to my soul, **saved me** from the pit of corruption, . . .

41:28—For I beheld, and there was no man; even among **men**, . . .

42:19—**For I will send my servant unto you who are blind; yea, a messenger to open the eyes of the blind, and unstop the ears of the deaf;**
42:20—**And they shall be made perfect notwithstanding their blindness, if they will hearken unto the messenger, the Lord's servant.**
42:21—Thou art a people. seeing many things, but thou observest not; opening the ears to hear, but thou hearest not.
42:22—**The Lord is not well pleased with such a people, but for his righteousness' sake he will magnify the law and make it honorable.**
42:23—**Thou art** a people robbed and spoiled; **thine enemies, all of them,** have snared thee in holes, and they have hid thee in prison houses; they have taken thee for a prey, and none delivereth; for a spoil, and none saith, Restore.
42:24—Who among **them** will give ear unto **thee,** or hearken and hear thee for the time to come? And who gave Jacob for a spoil,

King James Translation

42:24—Who gave Jacob for a spoil, and Israel to the robbers? did not the Lord, he against whom we have sinned? for they would not walk in his ways, neither were they obedient unto his law.

42:25—Therefore he hath poured upon him the fury of his anger, and the strength of battle: and it hath set him on fire round about, yet he knew not; and it burned him, yet he laid it not to heart.

43:13— . . . I will work and who shall let it?

44:21—Remember these, O Jacob and Israel; . . .

50:1—Thus saith the Lord, Where is the bill of your mother's divorcement, whom I have put away? or which of my creditors is it to whom I have sold you? Behold, for your iniquities have ye sold yourselves, and for your transgressions is your mother put away.

50:2—Wherefore, when came, was there no man? when I called, was there none to answer? Is my hand shortened at all, that it cannot redeem? or have I no power to deliver? behold, at my rebuke I dry up the sea, I make the rivers a wilderness: their fish stinketh, because there is no water, and dieth for thirst.

Inspired Version

and Israel to the robbers? did not the Lord, he against whom **they** have sinned?

42:25—For they would not walk in his ways, neither were they obedient unto his law: therefore he hath poured upon **them** the fury of his anger, and the strength of battle; and **they** have set **them** on fire round about, yet **they** know not, and it burned **them**, yet **they** laid it not to heart.

43:13— . . . I will work and who shall **hinder** it?

44:21— Remember **thee**, O Jacob and Israel; . . .

50:1—**Yea, for thus saith the Lord, Have I put thee away, or have I cast thee off for ever?** For thus saith the Lord, Where is the bill of your mother's divorcement? To whom have I put thee away, or to which of my creditors have I sold you; yea, to whom have I sold you?

50:2—Behold, for your iniquities have ye sold yourselves, and for your transgressions is your mother put away; wherefore, when I came there **was no man**; when I called **there was none to answer**. **O house of Israel**, is my hand shortened at all, that it cannot redeem; or have I no power to deliver?

50:3—Behold, at my rebuke I dry up the sea, I make their rivers a

King James Translation

50:3—I clothe the heavens with blackness, and I make sackcloth their covering.

50:4— . . . I should know how to speak a word in season to him that is weary: he wakeneth morning by morning, he wakeneth mine ear to hear as the learned.

50:5—The Lord God hath opened mine ear, . . .
50:8—He is near that justifieth me; . . .
. . . who is mine adversary? Let him come near to me.
50: 9—Behold, the Lord God will help me; who is he that shall condemn me? lo, they shall all wax old as a garment; the moth shall eat them up.

50:11—Behold, all ye that kindle a fire, . . .

51:1—Hearken to me, ye that follow after righteousness, ye that seek the Lord: look unto the rock whence ye are hewn, and to the hole of the pit whence ye are digged.

51:7— . . . the people in whose heart is my law; . . .

Inspired Version

wilderness; and their fish to stink, because the waters are dried up, and they die because of thirst. I clothe the heavens with blackness, and I make sackcloth their covering.

50:4. . . I should know how to speak a word in season **unto thee, O house of Israel, when ye are weary**. He waketh morning by morning, he waketh mine ear to hear as the learned.

50:5—The Lord God hath **appointed mine ears**, . . .
. . . and the Lord is near and he justifieth me.
50:6— . . . Who is mine adversary? Let him come near me, **and I will smite him with the strength of my mouth**; for the Lord God will help me; **and all they which shall condemn me**, behold all they shall wax old as a garment and the moth shall eat them up.

50:8—Behold all ye that **kindleth fire**, . . .

51:1—Hearken **unto** me, ye that follow after righteousness; ye that seek the Lord, look unto the rock **from** whence ye were hewn, and to the hole of the pit **from** whence ye are digged.

51:7— . . . the people in whose heart **I have written** my law; . . .

King James Translation

51:11— . . . and everlasting joy shall be upon their head:

51:12—I, even I, am he that comforteth you: who art thou . . .

51:19—These two things are come unto thee; who shall be sorry for thee? desolation, and destruction, and the famine, and the sword: by whom shall I comfort thee?

51 20—Thy sons have fainted, . . .

52 6— . . . therefore they shall know in that day that I am he that doth speak: . . .

52:7—How beautiful upon the mountains are the feet of him that bringeth good tidings, that publisheth peace; that bringeth good tidings of good, . . .

52:15—So shall he sprinkle many nations; . . .

54:10— . . . the covenant of my peace . . .

54:15—Behold, they shall surely gather together, but not by me: . . .

57:5— . . . under the clefts of the rocks?

60:22— . . . I the Lord will hasten it in his time.

62:4— . . . but thou shalt be called Hephzibah, and thy land Beulah: . . .

Inspired Version

51:11—. . . and everlasting joy **and holiness** shall be upon their **heads**; . . .

51:12—**I am he, yea**, I am he that comforteth you; **behold**, who art thou . . .

51:19—These **two** sons are come unto thee; **they** shall be sorry for thee, **thy** desolation, and destruction, and the famine, and the sword; **and** by whom shall I comfort thee?

51:20—Thy sons have fainted **save these two**, . . .

52:6— . . . **yea, in that day** they shall know that I am he that doth speak: . . .

52:7—**And then shall they say**, How beautiful upon the mountains are the feet of him that bringeth good tidings **unto them**, that publisheth peace; that bringeth good tidings **unto them** of good, . . .

52:15—So shall he **gather** many nations; . . .

54:10— . . . the covenant of my **people** . . .

54:15—Behold, they shall surely gather together **against thee**, but not by me; . . .

57:5— . . . under the **clefts** of the rocks?

60:22— . . . I the Lord will hasten it in **my** time.

62:4— . . . but thou shalt be called **Delightful**, and thy land **Union**; . . .

King James Translation

62:5—For as a young man marrieth a virgin, so shall thy sons marry thee . . .

63:17—O Lord, why hast thou made us to err from thy ways, and hardened our heart from thy fear? . . .

64:5—Thou meetest him that rejoiceth and worketh righteousness, those that remember thee in thy ways: behold, thou art wroth; for we have sinned: in those is continuance, and we shall be saved.
64:6—But we are all as an unclean thing, and all our righteousnesses are as filthy rags; . . .

65:1—I am sought of them that asked not for me; I am found of them that sought me not: I said, Behold me, behold me, unto a nation that was not called by my name.

65:2—I have spread out my hands all the day unto a rebellious people, which walketh in a way that was not good, after their own thoughts;

65:4— . . . which eat swine's flesh, and broth of abominable things is in their vessels;
65:20—There shall be no more thence an infant of days, . . .

Inspired Version

62:5—For as a young man marrieth a virgin, so shall thy **God** marry thee; . . .

63:17—O Lord, why hast thou **suffered us** to err from thy ways, and **to harden** our heart from thy fear? . . .

64:5—Thou meetest him that **worketh righteousness, and rejoiceth him that remembereth thee in thy ways; in righteousness there is continuance**, and **such** shall be saved.
64:6—**But we have sinned**; we are all as an unclean thing, and all our righteousnesses are as filthy rags; . . .

65:1—**I am found of them who seek after me, I give unto all them that ask of me; I am not found of them that sought me not, or that inquireth not after me.**
65:2—**I said unto my servant**, Behold me, **look upon me; I will send you unto** a nation that is not called after my name, for I have spread out my hands all the day to a people who walketh not in my ways, and their works are evil and not good, and they walk after their own thoughts.
65:4— . . . which eat swine's flesh, and broth of abominable **beasts, and pollute their vessels**;
65:20—**In those days** there shall be no more thence an infant of days, . . .

And the work of righteousness shall be peace; and the effect of righteousness quietness and assurance for ever.

And my people shall dwell in a peaceable habitation, and in sure dwellings, and in quiet resting places;

(Isaiah 32:17-18)

ABOUT THE AUTHOR

Duane S. Crowther is well-known and highly qualified as an author, scriptorian, theologian, and lecturer. He graduated with high honors from Brigham Young University with a B.A. in music education. He also holds a Masters Degree from Brigham Young University in Old and New Testament, an M.B.A. from the University of Phoenix, and has completed course work for a Ph.D. in music education at the University of Utah.

A creative and prolific author, Mr. Crowther has written more than forty books and over three dozen cassette talk tapes, plus numerous magazine articles. He is known for his writings on the scriptures and his indepth research in various fields including life-after-death experiences, the last days, the nature of revelation, the spiritual gifts, and LDS missionary and defense of the faith themes. His best-known books include *Prophecy—Key to the Future, The Prophecies of Joseph Smith, Gifts of the Spirit, Prophets and Prophecies of the Old Testament, Life Everlasting, Inspired Prophetic Warnings, How to Understand the Book of Mormon* and *Teaching Choral Concepts.*

In his professional life he has served as an LDS Seminary instructor and principal, taught university classes for the BYU, University of Utah and University of Phoenix, and has taught music in the public schools. He has owned and managed several book and music stores. For almost three decades he has been President and the Senior Editor of Horizon Publishers in Bountiful, Utah.

Mr. Crowther has written and produced patriotic pageants for the stakes in his area and has lectured at numerous business seminars, writers' seminars, BYU Education and Leadership Weeks, youth conferences and other Church and community gatherings. An accomplished musician, he has taught concert band, stage band, orchestra and directed various choirs in the public schools. He is a talented choral director and has directed a variety of community and church choirs, including the Delta Phi returned missionaries chorus at BYU, a SPEBSQSA barbershop chorus, a community girls chorus, and large ward, stake and regional choirs. His doctoral dissertation, a program for training school and church choirs, is used in thousands of high schools across the nation. He has composed several musical numbers and arranged others for choral performances.

The Crowthers enjoy travel and escorting travel tours. Together they have conducted and led several tours to Israel and various European and Middle-east countries. Mr. Crowther also has led groups to Hawaii and to Central America.

His has been a life of continued service within the Church, and he has served in many leadership and teaching positions. He is a Master M-Man and an Eagle Scout. He has filled three missions. He has been a District President, Branch President, High Priests Group Leader, Stake Mission President, Seventy's Quorum President, and Elders Quorum President. He also has served as a Sunday School Superintendent and President, a YMMIA Superintendent and President, a Ward Music Chairman, a Stake Music Director and Drama Director, a member of several stake boards, a director of stake and ward choirs, a Gospel Doctrine class instructor for many years, and has filled other callings as a teacher and teacher-trainer. Other Church assignments have included service as a temple worker in the Salt Lake Temple and service as a tour guide on Temple Square.

Mr. Crowther is married to the former Jean Decker, who is also an author and musician. They are the parents of eight children and reside in Bountiful, Utah.

INDEX

-A-

Adam-ondi-Ahman, Council at 147
Ahab 36,37, 40, 41, 43
Ahaz 15, 17, 18, 21, 42, 44, 48, 49, 51, 55, 68
Ahaziah 36, 41
Adad-nirari III 21, 32
Agency, nature of man's 126-129
Amaziah 17, 38, 41
Americas 78, 143
Amon 21
Amoz 15
Apostasy, first centuries A.D. 140
Ashurbanipal 35
Asshur 35
Asshur-Lush 33
Ashur-nasirpal II 32
Assur-Dayan III 21, 33
Assyrians, 185,000 43, 44
Athaliah 41
Azariah (see Amaziah)

-B-

Baasha 36
Battle of Armegeddon 84, 87, 151-152, 154
Battle of Gog and Magog 158
Battle of Ramoth-gilead 36, 37, 40
Bel 63

-L-

-M-

-N-

-O-

Trust ye in the LORD for ever: for in the LORD JEHOVAH is everlasting strength:

(Isaiah 26:4)